BUYING INTO ENGLISH

PITTSBURGH SERIES IN COMPOSITION, LITERACY, AND CULTURE

David Bartholomae and Jean Ferguson Carr, Editors

Buying into English

LANGUAGE AND INVESTMENT IN THE NEW CAPITALIST WORLD

Catherine Prendergast

UNIVERSITY OF PITTSBURGH PRESS

Published by the University of Pittsburgh Press, Pittsburgh, Pa., 15260

Copyright © 2008, University of Pittsburgh Press

Manufactured in the United States of America

Printed on acid-free paper

10 9 8 7 6 5 4 3 2 1

Library of Congress Cataloging-in-Publication Data

Prendergast, Catherine, 1968–

   Buying into English : language and investment in the new capitalist world /
Catherine Prendergast.

       p.   cm. — (Pittsburgh series in composition, literacy, and culture)

   Includes bibliographical references and index.

   ISBN-13: 978-0-8229-4346-4 (cloth : alk. paper)

   ISBN-10: 0-8229-4346-8 (cloth : alk. paper)

   ISBN-13: 978-0-8229-6001-0 (pbk. : alk. paper)

   ISBN-10: 0-8229-6001-X (pbk. : alk. paper)

   1. English language—Slovakia.   2. English language—Economic aspects—
Slovakia.   3. Intercultural communication—Slovakia.   4. English language—
Globalization.   5. Language and culture—Slovakia.   I. Title.

   PE2751.P74 2008

   427'.94373—dc22   2008004243

for John

Contents

Acknowledgments

The research for this book was funded by a Fulbright grant administered through the Council for International Exchange of Scholars. I am greatly indebted to the language faculty at Slovak Technical University for hosting me during the period of my research. The writing of this book was made possible by a sabbatical and by the enlightened parental leave program at the University of Illinois at Urbana-Champaign; the latter allowed me to continue to write while tending to my greatest joy and inspiration, my son, Sig. Colleagues who read portions of this work in draft form were generous with their time and comments: Dennis Baron, David Cooper, Debra Hawhee, Bruce Horner, Min-Zhan Lu, Martin Manalansan, Brian Schwegler, John Trimbur, and Evan Watkins. Great thanks are due numerous others: Rado Hrivnak and Maria Corejova, for translation; Zuzana Ličková and Monika Drinková, for Slovak lessons; Jan Adamcyzk of the University of Illinois Slavic and East European library, for uncovering the historical record; Lenka Fuchsová for fact-checking; Jessica Bannon, for cite checking; Carol Sickman-Garner, for telling me in the nicest ways what needed to go; Patrick Berry, for peerless developmental editing and technical assistance; Dave Bartholomae and Jean Ferguson-Carr, for their enthusiasm and vision. My writing partner, the brilliant and huge-hearted Nancy Abelmann, revealed the better book, word by word. Rebecca Holden, my traveling partner, read every page of an early draft, holding an infant Sig while I slept. Lastly, I cannot thank enough those who shared their stories, lives, food, and homes with me as they taught me lessons in how the world works that I could not have learned from books.

BUYING INTO ENGLISH

Introduction

THE FIRST LANGUAGE
OF CAPITALISM

For many in the world today, learning English is virtually a must. English has made an unprecedented rise to become the world's lingua franca, the most commonly used language of global trade. As such it has become the object of enormous investment, as eagerly sought as a piece of property or a hot stock. At the millennial moment, defined by global capitalism and the rise of the knowledge economy, people around the world are buying into English, investing their money and time in it, hoping for a favorable outcome.[1]

These investments are motivated by the common belief that English, as the language that allows for the free movement of people, goods, and services that characterizes globalization, is essential for developing countries to compete on a level playing field with developed ones. *Buying into English* questions that belief through a critical ethnographic study of a piece of the world where people are buying into English at a furious pace—the postcommunist state of Slovakia formed in 1993, after Czechoslovakia split into separate nations.[2] For Slovakia, a large part of the business of becoming a capitalist state was learning capitalism's first language: English. Before the Soviet Union's collapse, English language material was heavily censored by the government and English instruction limited due to the language's association with capitalist countries. Following Czechoslovakia's peaceful overthrow of the communist regime in the "Velvet Revolution" of 1989, however, English in Slovakia flourished, supported by a booming language teaching industry. In the space of little more than a decade, Slovaks went from very rarely hearing or using English in daily life to walking through shopping malls sporting English names, including one in the capital city of Bratislava whose corridors were dubbed "Wall Street" and "Fifth Avenue." English had made the leap from lingua non grata to lingua franca.

The English, the malls: the "real" Wall Street embraced both developments in Slovakia. In 2005 *Barron's* deemed Slovakia "central Europe's star reformer," a "hot spot for foreign direct investment," though with the caveat that mass proficiency in English would be instrumental to the country's sustaining its star status. The *New York Times* trumpeted, "Once a Backwater, Slovakia Surges," for an article that compared Slovakia's auspicious signs of development to those in Ireland two decades prior. The *Economist* declared, "The Slovaks have it right," namely, the ability to attract investment from richer countries by flaunting low labor costs while investing in education.[3] Even the World Bank sang the country's praises, rating Slovakia the top reformer in improving the climate for foreign investment.[4]

While these reports from the Western press suggest a somewhat uncomplicated transition out of communism, one brought about by the adoption of a slate of neoliberal economic reforms including corporate tax breaks and loosened labor codes, the stories of the individuals I spoke with in Slovakia, who learned and used English in the midst of this transition, belie this easy picture. They instead reveal the complexities of lives transformed in ways big and small by capitalism and its lingua franca. During the communist regime, Slovaks had looked forward to capitalism, equating it with freedom of choice, freedom of movement, and fully stocked stores. Capitalism when it came, of course, was somewhat more complicated than had been anticipated. Far from intuitive, capitalism in practice had to do some work to establish itself as the "common sense" of how to operate in the world,[5] and some form of English had equally to establish itself as the common sense of how to communicate in global capitalism. English lessons in postcommunist Slovakia thus conveyed the rudimentary logic of capitalism: how to shop, how to drive, and most of all how to learn ever more English to keep your job. "Father must learn English," one dialogue lesson in a Slovak-authored textbook proclaimed, in order to keep his job in the export division of his company. Quickly absorbing this and similar lessons, Slovaks began learning English en masse: They studied English while they were making breakfast, eating dinner, driving to work. Their children faced increasing English requirements in their schools. Teachers of Russian (communism's first language), suddenly no longer in demand once the Soviet-backed requirement was abolished, were requalified to teach English in two-year courses at the state's expense. Employers hired English teachers to instruct their entire staff, and people seeking better employment flocked to the new private language academies that had sprung up when the state monopoly on education expired. Albeit these new schools offered courses in many of the major languages of Western Europe, courses in English dominated and were sometimes more expensive. One school in 2003, for example, charged 8,200 Slovak crowns (then roughly 250 dollars) for forty-eight hours of business English, while charging only 3,000 crowns for fifty hours of business German; such price disparities were a quick lesson in English's centrality to capitalism.[6]

These many lessons in English, however, did not teach deeper logics of capitalism, including the fact that the global knowledge economy's reliance on information—finding it, peddling it, hiding it, distorting it—meant that English, fast becoming the ur-form of information, would always be manipulated and controlled by more powerful players in more powerful countries. English may have provided Slovaks a leg up; however, it also provided the terms through which they continued to be cast as "backward" in the development narrative, even as they joined the European Union and even as corporations of Western Europe, America, and Asia set up shop in Slovak towns where the labor force was educated and inexpensive. Slovaks were given a place in the global economy through English, but it was a sharply defined and decidedly second-class one.

Slovaks expressed their frustrations about their marginal place in the global economy in unofficial ways. A case in point: the 2004 article

"Tongue Surgery Is Necessary for Perfect English," in the online version of Slovakia's daily paper *Sme,* reported that some South Koreans have tongue surgery to improve their English pronunciation. The report sparked a lively discussion (in Slovak) on the daily's message board, as Slovaks wondered what their own English would get them in the global economy. One reader wrote to another that he would do better to take up Chinese rather than continue to pursue English, arguing, "Your English pronunciation would require tongue surgery anyway, as you're just a scum from the Eastern bloc. It's just that they won't tell you this openly because you're a good henchman and workhorse for them."[7]

This comment revealed capitalism's unspoken ("they won't tell you this"): entering the global economy was not about mastery of its putative terminology—English—but about negotiating the global order's asymmetries on a daily basis. In May 2004, one month after this article about tongue surgery appeared, Slovakia joined a European Union still much divided as Slovaks faced labor restrictions in a majority of the more established member states; outside of Europe, they continued to be subject to visa restrictions when traveling to the United States, unlike their fellow European Union members, the French, the Germans, and the Swedes. Eastern European workers were to be courted by multinational corporations on their own soil because they could be employed at lower wages than Western workers yet scrutinized—if not completely rejected—for attempting to move beyond their borders. Although Slovaks had yearned for the freedom of movement that the end of communism would bring, it became increasingly clear that it would be much easier for them to walk down shopping mall corridors in Bratislava named "Fifth Avenue" and "Wall Street" than it would be to walk down the actual streets. No amount of English fluency would allow Slovaks to completely transcend the dual designation the global economy had assigned them (as the reader of the tongue surgery report bluntly put it), of "scum from the Eastern bloc" and "workhorse." This most dispiriting of insights is one that did not hit Slovaks immediately with full force in 1989. Rather, it came to them as they acquired English and were thereby brought into the sweep of the world economy and its information networks. Even as the rise of the knowledge economy meant that opting out of English was not a possibility, the same economy dictated that English as lingua franca would ever be out of their control; English would never "work" for them in the same way it "worked" for developed nations. The primary English lesson that Slovaks learned was that the language was as likely to reinforce their marginal status as it was to assure their success.

Although such is the big picture of English in Slovakia, not everyone inhabits that big picture in the same way. Slovakia's attempt to demonstrate mass English proficiency inevitably breaks down into thousands of people learning English one by one. Each of these people is driven not only by global currents but also by local and even personal economies wherein intangibles like nostalgia, duty, and aesthetic preferences all express themselves. As I witnessed, English in Slovakia was refracted through people's experiences and imaginings. For most I spoke with who grew up during the communist regime, English meant something to them before they even learned it, but depending on the associations that English conjured in their minds, they gravitated toward different forms of English, looked to English to accomplish different things in their lives. As their lives changed, so did the English that they sought. The stories of this book further show that personal experiences during the postcommunist period could alter the form of English people embraced or rejected.

Taken collectively, however, these stories do suggest a common denominator to people's perceptions of English—that is, while English during the communist era was predominantly associated with freedom, afterward it was predominantly associated with money and influence. I want to be clear that English was associated with freedom during communism *not* because the language inherently carried that value or because England and America had succeeded in projecting that value. Slovaks associated English with freedom because under the communist regime the language was controlled and contained, rationed out to people in similar bondage. I believe that Slovaks felt a kinship with English during this period, one that led many of them to fight for English (though often unsuccessfully). After English became the lingua franca, the language that was unavoidable rather than the language that was limited, they would fight to mark a place for themselves in the world in English, often by appropriating it in artful ways. My interlocutors often repurposed different regional expressions and proverbs to describe their experience with English, but significantly they did not all reach for the same expression; various personal desires and histories continued to animate English even at the moment of capitalist integration. Constantly under pressure to master more or different English to meet specific needs of the global information economy, Slovaks answered with their own language games. Puns, innuendo, black humor—such were the idioms and gestures giving life to English in the postcommunist era in Slovakia. These expressions signify that Slovaks understood very well that in the global economy it would matter more who was speaking English, not how well it was spoken.

THE ECONOMY OF ENGLISH

The Slovak experience has great implications for understanding both English as a lingua franca and the causes of persistent inequities in the post–Cold War global economy. English has frequently been likened to a form of currency, one that can help markets function best for all participants by serving as a neutral medium for exchange. Hence the 1998 call in *Business Communication Quarterly* for English teachers to develop "a kind of common currency for global knowledge production and exchange." And hence the 2005 observation of a commentator in the *Financial Times* that "being a native speaker [of English] is like possessing a reserve currency."[8] The currency analogy is given fullest breadth by linguist Robert Phillipson, who compares money and languages explicitly. Both, Phillipson argues, are systems of exchange and accounting as well as storehouses of values, whether those values are monetary or cultural.[9] However, such analogies fail to capture fully the complexities of English at work in the knowledge economy.

The global knowledge economy is driven not so much by cash moving things as by the generation and manipulation of information. Linguist David Crystal's study of the rise of global English recognizes the centrality of English to this new economy. Crystal argues that American dominance of the growing banking sector after World War I raised English's global profile because foreign investment was largely to be supported by American financial institutions. Making clear the link between the knowledge economy, credit, and the preeminence of English, Crystal explains: "'Access to knowledge' now became 'access to knowledge about how to get financial backing.' If the metaphor 'money talks' has any meaning at all, those are the days in which it was shouting loudly—and the language in which it was shouting was English."[10]

As Crystal suggests, knowledge has always been crucial to any kind of production. Economists tell us, however, that once an economy runs on investments and loans, equity and credit, knowledge becomes more centrally the object of production rather than a means to it. Economists Joseph E. Stiglitz and Bruce Greenwald explain that the granting of a loan, for example, entails the costly process of producing specific information about specific institutions or people. Likewise, to invest (with any hope of success) in a stock, one generally has to collect more specific information than the price of the share. As an industry emerges around knowledge production and circulation, only new information—or at least *seemingly* new information—sells, as old information is of little value to investors.[11]

All manufacturers attempt minor innovations (or at least the appearance of innovation) to their products to boost sales, of course, and all hide information critical to production to maintain their competitive edge. But the corporate scandals around the millennium—those that made Enron, MCI, and Martha Stewart front-page news—demonstrated the crucial place of information in the economy in that all were cases in which certain parties generated profit by ensuring they had the right information, while other people had erroneous or outdated information. All involved the hiding, distorting, or hoarding of information, resulting in what economists would call "information asymmetry."[12] To be sure, the economy is also characterized by information asymmetry that does not cross the boundary of legality. Companies try not to disclose more than they must to investors or customers and are adept at manipulating language to manage the information in mandatory disclosures.[13] Information asymmetry is, as Stiglitz argues, business as usual in capitalism.

The concept of information asymmetry is, I offer, a more apt economic metaphor than currency to understand the significance of English to today's global economy. Consider again the reports from *Barron's* and the *Economist* about Slovakia. These press accounts collectively form a discourse in the global lingua franca of English that compares Slovakia to other emerging markets for an audience of investors. Buying *Barron's,* the *Economist,* or the *New York Times,* the English speaking investor is hoping to have purchased the good news: when will Slovakia *become* Ireland, and how can I find out before others? With this investor-reader in mind, the *Barron's* article ends with a list of funds that will allow one to take advantage of Slovakia's surge. The information in these press reports is in essence the commodity of the new economy, an economy in which English has become virtually unavoidable.[14]

Because English has become so central to participation in the global marketplace, people in newly capitalist countries have had little choice but to throw themselves into learning it; as a result, an industry emerged to accommodate their new "need." The boom in English instruction in Slovakia accordingly took on the particular contours of the rapidly shifting knowledge economy, generating courses in different forms of English to fit the newest economic trends. To stay marketable in the growing field of competitors, English continually had to be "remade." Niche versions of English proliferated: courses entitled "English for Mechanical Engineers" and "English for Au Pairs" took their place next to generic business English courses, promising a quick path to the jobs as auto engineers and domestics for which Slovaks had been pegged. It didn't matter that Slovak women had been successfully operating as au pairs in Western European countries for years before these courses appeared (indeed, the rationale au pair agencies historically used to attract young women was that the experience itself would improve their language skills). Suddenly, there was a special English to be learned, a credential that could be attained to give someone a boost in the market. People had to weigh what brand of English to learn (or teach) and had to pursue English as a shifting target. Learning English became, as one of my interlocutors put it, a "never-ending story." Much like buying the "right" stock, buying into English entailed risk and dependence, often on questionable forms of knowledge generated by interested parties.

If, as the Enrons of the world have shown us, money is to be made from keeping information as asymmetrical as possible, in a knowledge economy in which English is the lingua franca, money is to be made by making communication in English as asymmetrical—as fraught with distortions and complications—as possible. Misunderstandings are certainly an unavoidable feature of communication, but another feature of communication is that those with more money and influence have the lux-

ury of being misunderstood while those with less do not.[15] Here is where
Slovaks occupied the downside of routine acts of communication in the
global lingua franca. Each "misunderstanding" in English generally bore
consequences for them in terms of lost jobs, lost contacts, lost dignity, or
diminished political clout, particularly as it reinforced their position as
second-class citizens of the global order and, simultaneously, the preemi-
nent value of some elusive English. Despite ever more specialized English
knowledge, ever more certification, Slovakia's position as "developing"
(with all the perpetuity of process that the suffix -ing suggests) continually
put Slovaks in a disadvantaged position in their communications with any
of the wealthier and more established countries of the West.

This position was one that the Slovaks I spoke with in 2003 were finding burdensome. I frequently heard variations of the question, "What does
the West want from us?" Of course, the one thing that had remained clear
throughout is that the countries of the West wanted to maintain their economic advantages in the global economy; they were eager for emerging
markets in which to invest but less keen on having those markets turn
into genuine competition. Slovaks in the international business realm
were particularly aware that Slovakia's growth threatened "old" EU member states (such as France and Germany) that were experiencing their own
political and economic woes. Several of the Slovaks I met remarked on the
sometimes lackluster economic performance of their Western neighbors
and worried that the economic mandates issued from the offices of the EU
for new member states were primarily designed to protect the West from
losing investment and jobs to the East. Many Slovaks felt that the EU's restrictions seemed incompatible with capitalism's official orthodoxy of liberalism; the EU's bureaucracy seemed contrary to the "common sense" of
capitalism as they understood it and more in keeping with communism's
myriad and arbitrary restrictions. To them, success in capitalism should
involve simply good ideas and the grit to make them work. They wondered
if the East shouldn't be teaching the West about capitalism instead of the
other way around. They wondered if in the end the world they were joining
would be greatly different from the world they thought they had left.

The economics of English revealed through the Slovak situation suggest that the lingua franca is language as battlefield; it is the terrain upon
which players in the global information economy grapple for property, re-

spectability, and political voice. That English had become this terrain was a circumstance about which Slovaks repeatedly voiced ambivalence. Their acknowledgment that English had made it to the top of the linguistic pile was frequently followed by a qualification: "for better or worse," "fortunately or unfortunately," "unfortunately or thank God."

Ethnography, it has been observed, allows us a view from the ground of the paradoxes, contradictions, and ambiguities of change in postcommunist states.[16] It presents this "ground" through the filter of the ethnographer's necessarily limited vision, of course—in this case, my perception as a foreigner to Slovakia, an American with a history of my own engagements with the English industry in the country, which I discuss below. To my mind, the greatest paradox I encountered is that when people invest in English, they do so with some hope but by no means complete faith in the development narrative. This mixture of hope and doubt is first introduced here through the conjunction of a few stories drawn from my observations, interviews, and personal experiences. These stories trouble the narrative of English's uncomplicated role in global progress suggested by *Barron's* and similar reports.

A TALE OF TWO THANK YOU'S

I first taught English in Slovakia in 1992. Looking for a summer break from graduate school, a friend and I sought a location where our services would be in demand but where we could also afford to live. Through letter correspondence, we were hired by the director of a new private summer program in Bratislava for high school students. The director asked us to bring all our teaching materials, because none existed for the new brand of English he was selling: colloquial and idiomatic American English language and culture. We set off with lesson plans designed around baseball, tongue twisters, American folk songs, and the Fourth of July.

Although the course had the flavor of a cultural exchange, a "thank you" letter I received at the course's end outlined Slovakia's great expectations for development and lay bare the stakes of our students' labors. The letter of July 14, 1992, praised my "highly competitive teaching performance" and described my participation as a "meritful deed," which had contributed to "breaking the recent artificial barrier" and also aided "our people's gradual return to the free world where we hope to thrive not only in economics, but in international human relations in the foreseeable future." It closed, "Dear American friend, we do hope to meet you some day again."

It would be difficult to imagine any American working today in Slovakia's busy capital city so lauded. However, when I taught this summer course, I was the first American many of my students had met. I was employed specifically because I was considered a "native" speaker of American English, so the students could hear the "real thing." Before 1989, students had had little opportunity to converse with English or American citizens and very little opportunity to be taught by them.[17] Yet in 1992, each of my students had taken the step of paying for extra English courses to learn distinctly American conversational English, even though their opportunities to use the idioms we proffered might be rare.

We returned to teach the summer course again in 1994. In the years since our first visit, Slovakia had achieved independent statehood, and we were no longer notable as arbiters of American culture or conversational English. By the 1994–95 school year, approximately 80 percent of pupils in secondary schools in Slovakia were learning English, often from British or American nationals sent by the Peace Corps, Education for Democracy, or another Western agency.[18] Our new students were approaching us with the lyrics of current American songs, asking us what they meant. In 1992, we had brought the script of a play for them to perform; in 1994, they chose to write an episode based on the American series *The Streets of San Francisco,* which was at that time in heavy rotation on one of the local television networks.

I returned again to Slovakia in 2003 to investigate the effects of the global English education boom, of which I had been just one small part. Slovakia, in the meantime, had become a classic case of "macroaquisition," which defines a group's effort to acquire a language.[19] The dictates of the global economy meant that the English learning environment I had stepped into in the early 1990s was gone. English was no longer a perk; it had become an imperative. No one was selling lessons in baseball, tongue twisters, and the Fourth of July. Instead, I was asked by the mechanical engineering faculty at a technical university to teach a class on the modern cover letter and CV—genres that had altered radically when the fall of the Soviet regime meant competition for jobs.

Students had changed a great deal as well in the near decade since I had last visited, having had in some cases firsthand experiences of living abroad. At the end of my lesson on CVs and cover letters (which included some discussion of what was meant by volunteer experience—a construct that the class puzzled over at some length, as the idea of work that was both unpaid and authorized didn't translate very well), a student who had spent a year of high school in California asked, "What about thank you letters?" I asked, "What about them?" He responded, "You should tell them about them." This student stood out from many of his peers, looking from his hairstyle to his manner of dress as if he should have been in my classroom in America.[20] Yet his speaking for his peers, and his belief that there was some knowledge about the workings of capitalism encoded in English that they desperately needed to have, suggested that a reading of this student as merely "Westernized" would be glib, unless being "Westernized" entails an acute sense of the deficits of being regarded in business settings as "Eastern European." His comment demonstrated the notion that "marketing oneself is marketing the nation," a point made by Jonathan Larson in his study of the CV in Slovakia. Larson found that the CV had become such a crucial genre for Slovaks to learn because it contributed to an image of Slovakia as "translatable, and ultimately worthy of trust in investment."[21] The student I encountered knew that Slovaks, represented through the CV, would not easily "translate" into the global economy, or into English, on the same terms as Western students. They would have to go the extra mile to earn trust. He hoped the CV, plus the postinterview thank you letter, might give his classmates an edge to confront the derision they were likely to face.

JOZEF AND THE "SO-CALLED REVOLUTION"

The above incidents reveal that in postcommunist Slovakia, the understanding of what English "counts" changed greatly in the space of about a decade. A final story of English and the market provides an even sharper view of how Slovaks invested in English to learn the tricks of the global trade, only to find out that one of those tricks was that English was never enough.

Jozef invested great amounts of time in English (he had virtually no money to invest) in his hope against hope that he could win a job as a

European Union administrator for Slovakia. Having heard about my research through a friend on the faculty of the technical university hosting
me, he asked me to interview him so he could practice for the oral portion
of the upcoming exam required of all applicants for EU administrator positions. To prepare for the written portion of the exam, Jozef sat daily for
weeks at the library's Internet stations—from morning until four in the
afternoon—reading English texts on the Web site of the EU's personnel
selection office. Despite these efforts, he was nevertheless perplexed by the
impending exam: what the EU might be looking for he had no idea, but
he knew that knowledge of English would be instrumental to the process
of getting a job, as the test had to be taken in one of the EU's official languages—there were eleven at that point—and English was the one that
he knew best.

Jozef, who had rarely traveled outside of Slovakia, considered himself
the longest of shots for an administrator position. A self-described "free-
lancer," Jozef had some years back been let go—unjustly, he felt—from
his lecturing post at an art university in Bratislava, an event that precipi-
tated his bid for EU employment. Jozef's motivations for applying for the
job were primarily political rather than economic (even though the position of EU administrator paid an astronomical salary—the lowest available positions paid more than 2,000 euro a month—in comparison to the
less than 400 euro a month Slovak lecturers at universities earned).[22] His
pursuit of English was driven by the desire to gain the political voice he
felt he had been denied all his life, even into the present; his interview
provided a catalog of pre- and postrevolution suppressions.

A child of the Cold War and Soviet influence in Czechoslovakia, Jozef
was born in 1954 in historic Banská Štiavnica in the Slovak mountains,
site of the first European technical college. In high school a few years after
the Warsaw Pact invasion of Czechoslovakia in 1968, Jozef remembers a
day when he and his classmates were directed by the teacher to rip from
their textbooks a story by Alexander Solzhenitsyn, by then a denounced
dissident. He studied English in high school from 1970 until 1974, learning vocabulary and the fundamentals of grammar, as well as old English
folk songs including "John Brown's Body" and "My Bonnie Lies over the
Ocean." He considered this training a mere "formality." Echoing so many
others I spoke with, he laid the blame for the paucity of "active English"

instruction available to him on the influence of the communist regime: "There was no motivation or need for an active and regular English because there was no possibility to travel abroad, especially to the West, especially for people who were not involved in any communist power structures." Nonetheless, in college and following, Jozef discovered his own need for English as he became consumed with a question: "What is art?" A few books related to his specialty were available in the university library in English, and he sought them out. He described his relationship to English as "ad hoc . . . from 1974 until the so-called revolution. Only after the so-called revolution I tried to handle with English more regularly and more systematically."

The phrase "so-called revolution" struck me from the very first time Jozef used it in the interview. Jozef had earlier referred to the "so-called grammar school" he had attended, so initially I thought he used the qualifier "so-called" to mark a foreign expression or to indicate a proper noun, as did many Slovaks.[23] However, "so-called revolution" came up with startling consistency. He continued: "After the so-called revolution, I worked as an assistant professor at the Academy of Arts at the department for film and television theory at film faculty." I wanted to ask about his consistent use of the phrase "so-called revolution," but I didn't want to interrupt. When I broached the question of why he was taking the EU administrator test, however, it came back again: "Perhaps I could try to explain my way, how I could get from history and philosophy of art to European administration, because I think it might seem a little different, a little far from each other and a little inconsistent at the first view. But it's a longer story. Of course the most intrinsic issue of my interest is and remains the theory and philosophy of art. . . . As I tried to explain to people what art is, similarly I desired to teach, but it wasn't possible in the communist time because I had some problems with the communists and with the ideologies, but after *so-called revolution,* some revolutionary students invited me to teach at that academy of art." At this point, Jozef believed he could really make some changes to pedagogy as usual in the art academy. Having experienced very little choice of subjects in his schooling, Jozef was determined that the "so-called revolution" called for a revision of the curriculum so that students could assemble their own course of study. He was blocked, however, in the full execution of his plans by what he described as a "communist mafia and pack": "I succeeded to put such a [curricular] system at our department of film and television theory, but after several years when the communists saw that they have no need to be afraid and nothing will happen with them, there were more and more conflicts between our department of film and television theory and the other departments . . . because every department was occupied by a communist mafia and pack."

At this point in the interview, I was becoming more and more certain that the use of "so-called" as a qualifier for "revolution" was ironic. I interrupted what had been so far an uninterrupted narrative:

> ME: You said a number of times the "so-called revolution." Now when we say "so-called" we mean that we don't think, for example, that there was a revolution. Is that what you meant?
>
> JOZEF: Yes, yes, just so.
>
> ME: That nothing has changed.
>
> JOZEF: Nothing has changed, in fact.

As Jozef saw it, the same "pack" of communists that kept him from teaching before 1989 was still in power, laying roadblocks to any revision of the curriculum that would give students freedom of choice. After six years at the academy, his appointment was not renewed. Jozef looked for other ways to pursue educational reform, from the top rather than from the bottom. He worked for several years in a division of the Slovak Ministry of Education, where he tried to advance legislation for educational reform but found himself blocked once again: "No one has the interest to change. The other way around. They want only to keep the structures." His experience led him to consider what legislation might be advanced on the European level; thus he submitted the application to become a European Union administrator. He was concerned, though, that even if he passed the written test, including the multiple choice portion, he would be faced with an interview for which he felt completely unprepared. Having had few opportunities for what he called "active" use of English, he was terrified at the prospect of an interview. Indeed, I later realized, looking back over his interview, that he had shifted every question of mine back to the narrative of his move toward the EU, practicing for the upcoming interview he imagined with EU officials.

I met with Jozef a few times after our initial interview. He admitted that speaking with me for nearly two hours in English had been difficult and exhausting; it had taken him a full day in bed to recover from it. "It was something like a brain fever," he explained. We met again after the written portion of the EU administrator test itself, and he showed me a copy of the exam. The full-day written exam had apparently been even more torturous than his interview with me, requiring days of recovery. When it turned out that he had passed the multiple choice portion of the exam, he was jubilant. This meant that the test committee would read the essay he had written in English about his ideas for changing the European Union's approach to education. He was excited that he was one step further along in the application process, leaving only the interview (interviews would be conducted with only fifty of the original one thousand–plus applicants).

Including Jozef, I had spoken with or extensively interviewed five people who had registered to take the administrator examination for the EU. Four of them (all university lecturers like Jozef) hadn't studied and didn't expect to get past the multiple choice portion; indeed, they did not. Of all five, only Jozef's essay would be read. Some days before the exam, he sent me a draft of what he planned to write, a treatise on the failings of the circulation of knowledge in the global economy. His essay describes education in Slovakia as a monopoly, a "distortion of the open and free competition market" that "reminds of the conviction of the communists they are the extra wise 'people of the extra stamp' who can and must 'scientifically manage' and 'plan' all the production and decide about all the qualities, values, and prices and all the needs of the consumers and people." In other words, he was equating communism's centrally planned economy and its inherent hypocrisies with the EU's treatment of education in the knowledge economy. He charged that the European Union, despite its embrace of open and free competition, and despite its embrace of the "knowledge-based economy," seemed "unconcerned" with addressing the monopoly in the area of knowledge production—it only seemed concerned with the old commodities: "meat and grain, steel and coal."

Jozef's essay did not win him an interview for the position of EU administrator, perhaps unsurprisingly, as the essay boldly charges that the capitalism practiced by the EU is not free-market or liberal enough but is startlingly rather like the communism he had left not far enough behind. He felt that if the EU really took a knowledge-based economy seriously, students should have a choice of subjects to learn, just as they had a choice of products to buy. Jozef here was taking the logic of capitalism—its emphasis on choice and on the market as the ideal instrument for guaranteeing that choice—on its face terms. He saw such logic operating selectively in the West's treatment of Slovakia, writing that the allure the East held for the West was simply based on the East's cheap labor that the West could use.

I got the impression after I read the essay that Jozef didn't so much care whether or not it would get him the job; when he gave me the draft, he told me that regardless of the question, he would write that particular essay, imagining that the topics given would be broad enough to allow for it. After I returned to the United States, my sense of Jozef's intent was verified in an email he wrote, one year after I asked him how the test had turned out—when (as he put it) he felt himself at last ready to talk about it without anger. He reflected on the essay that ended his prospects with the EU: "I could not do it in any other way. For me, it was not a matter of 'getting job,' but it was a matter of trying to put certain 'reformist' ideas about education through with the help of EU—the 'reformist' ideas I cannot put through in Slovakia. But, when I see the European clerks are not interested in these 'my' ideas, the job of the 'European administrator' is apparently not the good way to try it and apparently not the good job for me." Recall that Jozef's initial excitement about the prospect of getting the position had been tinged with fatalism. He didn't think himself likely to be selected ultimately, but further, he worried that even should he make it to the EU, his previous experiences with bureaucratic regimes would be repeated on the supranational governmental level. He said in one of our discussions prior to the exam: "I hope that Europe can help us [to liberalize education], but perhaps I am very naive. . . . Perhaps also the European administration is also only a big bureaucratic mill where I would be only a very little wheel, but what I can do except to hope and to look for any possibilities?" He didn't think he was alone in his pessimism, and my interviews with Slovaks suggested that in fact he was not; for many I spoke with, whose experiences follow in the pages of this book, capitalism in practice seemed to have triumphed over communism only by incorporating communism's failings of bureaucracy and cronyism. Rather than serving as a path out of this trap, English had become "the extra stamp," another bureaucratic hurdle to ensure that vital information would remain fully available only to a select well-placed few. Jozef remarked of the general ennui greeting the fourteenth anniversary of the "so-called revolution" in Slovakia, "When even I, an anti-communist, am disillusioned, imagine the normal person."

ENGLISH HAS NO "HUMAN FACE"

At base this book is about hope—mentioned twice in the letter written to me by my employer in 1992, several times in my interviews with Jozef, continually in my research with Slovaks learning and using English. Hope, while intangible, is not inconsequential. Hope is a necessary precondition (along with information and resources) that allows people to make investments that in turn affect economies.[24] The hope that Jozef and my employer described reflected the great expectations that accompanied the country's journey out from under the communist regime and how "buying into English" in ways both material and psychological was central in meeting and too often disappointing those expectations.

Perhaps in recognition of the hope displayed by people in economically disadvantaged countries, organizations such as the World Bank and the UN, corporations such as Novartis, and world leaders including former President Bill Clinton have called for "globalization with a human face."[25] This phrase has become the rallying cry for those seeking to ensure that the needs of individuals throughout the world are considered in a process that is too often dominated by discussions about profits. To the extent that efforts to reform global capitalism lead to greater transparency of corporate and government activities, they can only be applauded. But appeals to humanness alone are unlikely to persuade multinational corporations, as the main agents of global capitalism, to act more ethically. Banks are, after all, in the business of trying to get to know the "human" side of their borrowers so they can gain more information about them and thereby assess their risks with greater accuracy.[26] In other words, emphasizing the "human" side of economics does not necessarily elicit altruistic urges to curb predatory capitalism, because such "human" accounts provide far more information on which to potentially capitalize than do the numbers alone.

There is a further problem with the phrase "globalization with a human face" that is particular to Slovakia: the notion of having an economic system with a "human face" cannot help but invoke Alexander Dubček's—the president of Czechoslovakia (and a Slovak)—coining of the phrase "socialism with a human face" to describe his attempt to ease political and cultural restrictions in the late 1960s. What followed was a disaster—the Soviet occupation of 1968—whose scope has touched every Slovak alive. The aim of this book is to appreciate the ambiguities that result from the collision of global economics, national history, and personal desires, *not* to put a human face on the ascendancy of English (one wonders which face would do) but to note that more than the equitable distribution of English is needed to address global inequities.

That the phrase "with a human face" attaches itself so easily to the notion of globalization, however, suggests the degree to which discussions of globalization (and I would include here discussions of global English) have emanated from a sensibility that does not take into account the histories of postcommunist nations. Much of the scholarly work on the spread of English has been concerned with defining the effects of linguistic imperialism related to British and American colonial and neocolonial activity.[27] What I offer here is a look at English from the other side of the Cold War, one that examines first the effects of Soviet imperialism on English and English language learners before considering the impact of the current forces of globalization.

SOME WORDS ON METHOD

This project developed over a considerable length of time, beginning with notes on my teaching from the early 1990s—written at that time without the certainty that they would ever be more than notes—and moving toward a more structured ethnographic study. At the center of this effort are twenty-five extensive semistructured interviews, one to two hours in length, that I conducted primarily with Slovaks who knew English but also with key figures in the English industry in Slovakia, including foreign teachers, journalists, and textbook authors.[28] These interviews were sometimes discrete encounters nested within longer-term relationships with former students, with colleagues with whom I worked in 2003, but also notably with friendship networks centered around two couples.

I stopped at twenty-five extensive interviews not because it was a goal I had originally set myself but because while details of individuals' experiences varied, the general contours of English in Slovakia had emerged and, as the interviews went on, did not alter greatly. I suspect, however, that had I interviewed ethnic Romany citizens of Slovakia, pensioners who didn't speak English, or ethnic Hungarians, I might have seen a different side of English's relationship to economic enfranchisement, one complicated by the social and economic marginalization of these groups.

In addition to the extensive interviews, the data that comprise this book emerged from daily observations, shorter conversations, and archival research. I consulted numerous Slovaks, both English speaking and not with specific questions—for example, about politics during the communist regime, the recent reform of the secondary school graduation exam, using English on the job, or why they had never learned English at all. I visited schools in different cities in Slovakia to observe English instruction in the classroom. I took field notes on the uses of English in public places, businesses, and the press.

A large part of the research for this book involved reviewing textbooks used in Slovakia for the teaching and learning of English. I wanted to get a sense of how these textual materials had changed over time, particularly from communism to postcommunism. Samples of newer textbooks were readily available: by 2003, most bookstores in Bratislava boasted a substantial inventory. Although I did not buy all of them (that would have entailed acquiring whole shelves of books), I took care to purchase those that my interlocutors mentioned using, those that I saw in use in schools or in homes, and those invoked at a meeting I attended of teachers and administrators engaged in rewriting the national secondary school graduation exam in English (the subject of chapter 4). Older textbooks, those that were published before 1989, were not available for sale, at least not in their original and unrevised editions. I asked those interlocutors who had learned English before 1989 to show me their textbooks, if they still had them (most did not); I found more textbooks at Slovakia's Pedagogical Library in Bratislava. Because the textbooks I reviewed attest to general shifts in the way English was taught pre- and post-1989, I have included excerpts from them as illustrations in the following chapters. In chapter 1, which discusses the experience of those people who learned English during the communist regime, illustrations are given from the pre-1989 textbooks. In chapter 3, which looks at English language and use at the moment of capitalist integrations, illustrations from post-1989 textbooks are provided. The reader may note that these illustrations sometimes directly and sometimes indirectly comment on the profile under discussion in the section in which they appear. I invite readers to draw their own connections between the particularities of the oral reports of learning English and the peculiar expressions and preoccupations of textbooks of the time.

One limitation on the research for this book was that imposed by my limited knowledge of the Slovak language, which includes reading ability and the ability to participate in routine conversation but falls far short of fluency. Where I conducted my own translations of texts appearing here, I checked the meaning with at least one other bilingual Slovak and English speaker. For longer documents and those involving more colloquial Slovak expressions (e.g., those used in the posts to the message board recorded in the introduction), I employed a Slovak-English translation service.

All extensive interviews were conducted in English, though occasionally short observations were made in Slovak that I later translated. Since the goal of my research was to examine the impact of English on people's lives, I used the ability to participate in an interview in English as the qualification for the interview itself. Conducting interviews entirely in English on the one hand constrained the range of expression of my interviewees. On the other hand, my own language deficiencies allowed for a mobilization of their in-progress English speaking subjectivities, sometimes as dry runs for encounters that the new world would demand (as with Jozef, the EU administrator aspirant), sometimes as flights of nostalgia into encounters with English for which the new world no longer provided much space. As many indicated, the English required in the interview with a "native" speaker provided an occasion to try out expressions long left behind in their present—to them, cramped—uses of English.

Ethnography is partial, consisting of stories delivered with all the exaggerations and peculiarities of the individual account and all the ethnographer's perceptual limitations. Where the accounts I collected differ from those of another source, I have noted this. However, ethnography, particularly one focusing on language, is more about the fact that experiences of reality and the expressions of those experiences differ than it is about uncovering a universal truth. My interlocutors conveyed their stories of English in their own Englishes. The words they chose reflected the Englishes they had learned and that they, with varying degrees of enthusiasm and ambivalence, embraced. Beyond clarifying meaning where necessary, I did not attempt to ascertain the "correct" form of their English speech, nor did I presume what they "actually" might have meant in Slovak. Their expressions, in other words, have no fixed, historically transcendent translation either into an imagined standard English or into an imagined standard Slovak. Linguistic fixity is the promise the global economy makes but never fulfills, which is ultimately the point of this book.

1   Lingua Non Grata
ENGLISH DURING COMMUNISM

> It is, of course, extremely difficult to grasp the
> historic quality of a moment when a global attack on
> the very notion of history is taking place, because it
> means trying to tell the story of the loss of story.
> —Václav Havel, *Open Letters: Selected Writings,*
>   *1965–1990*

BRATISLAVA, AUGUST 1994

English was coming through my window. Jan stood outside the house next to his girlfriend and his BMW, calling to me to hurry because everyone was waiting at the restaurant and hungry.

It seemed to me that somewhere between my visits to Slovakia in 1992 and 1994, Jan and his BMW had materialized along with diet soft drinks and the border between the Czech and Slovak Republics. I initially found him unnerving because he seemed ostentatious; he liked to get to know people by doing extravagant favors for them that would entail putting his possessions and social networks to visible work.

On this occasion, for example, Jan was driving me out of the city for dinner in *the car:* "Do you like it? Here, let me open the door for you."

And off we drove in one of the few Western brand names in plain sight. Almost five years after the fall of the communist regime, advertising was still rare enough in Slovakia that one product could easily capture the public space through a concerted blitz, or such seemed the strategy of one Western ice cream corporation, whose billboard advertisement was plastered every few hundred feet along the highway on our way out of town. As advertising goes, the billboard was not very conceptual—a shot of a prepackaged cone beside a smiling couple and Bratislava's blocklike fortress. Not shown were the miles of even more blocklike communist-built flats in Petržalka, located across the river from the fortress, nor the "New Bridge" (Nový Most), a relic of the Soviet occupation poised like a praying mantis over the Danube.

As we moved away from both fortress and flats, skirting the foothills of the Carpathians, heading into the vineyards of the fertile Danube river valley region, Jan turned to the backseat (his girlfriend was driving) and continued talking about cars.

"Do you know about the Chrysler version?" he asked. I feebly offered a car name. "No, you do not know it." He spelled the name of the car in the NATO phonetic alphabet, then segued into a short disquisition on pilot language before arriving at the rules of cockney rhyming slang.

We rounded a corner quickly, returning us conversationally to cars: "You know, that was a little fast for that curb, it's true, and a normal car would have gone into a skid, but not this BMW. She's specially designed to hold corners, even in the rain. Is BMW still a status symbol in America?"

After the trout dinner that Jan wouldn't let anyone pay for—my Slovak crowns came whizzing back across the table to the tune of the colloquially appropriate "What is this, three lousy bucks?"—we drove home, this time with Jan at the wheel. As we approached the outskirts of Bratislava, we passed shoes, then skidmarks, then a body stretched out on the side of the road under a sheet. Jan turned down Pink Floyd's *Animals* on the stereo to offer a commentary, again about cars: "You can tell the driver was going very fast. There were shoes in the road about fifty meters in front of the body. The car must have just knocked him out of his shoes and dragged him that far. If the car had had antilock brakes, like this one, it would not have happened."

"I can be very arrogant," Jan offered during one of our 2003 interviews as a matter-of-fact observation. He was responding to my admission that when I had first met him, I didn't know what to make of him. He had seemed in 1994 to be almost a parody of a new capitalist, his car then not merely newer, faster, and sleeker but a solution to the problem of unnecessary early road death. When we met again after the millennium, he was building a custom car and owned several BMWs, a Nissan Pathfinder complete with winch for off-roading trips to the Czech Republic, and (with a partner) a fleet of about one hundred rental cars. The corporate law firm he had cofounded in 1989, specializing in tax shelters and international mergers, had made him a lot of money; his knowledge of English, of which he was very proud, was no small part of his work. He had been the most proficient Slovak speaker of English I happened to meet in 1994;[1] that proficiency—and his wealth—had made him both anomaly and precursor of the times to come. By 2003, BMWs, SUVs, and other abbreviations for discretionary income were outpacing aging Škodas on the Bratislava hills, and fluent English was coming out of the mouths of shop clerks.

It's possible that having "made it," financially and linguistically, faster than so many others accounted for Jan's arrogance; however, as I talked to him, I came to understand that his demeanor formed a rebuke to the arrogance embodied by the totalitarian regime in power when he grew up. His love of English—and cars—was nurtured through a life wherein such things were not to hold a claim on one's attention, must less affection. English, pre-1989, in the area of Czechoslovakia that would later become Slovakia, was a language whose instruction and use had been contained due to its associations with capitalist countries. The containment of English became particularly pronounced during the period Jan and other people profiled in this chapter were attempting to acquire the language. When Russia and the other countries of the Warsaw Pact invaded Czechoslovakia on August 21, 1968, to quash the experiment in liberalized socialism known as the Prague Spring, the country entered a period of rigorous oppression and increased separation from the West known as "normalization." The purpose of "normalization" was to bring the country back to purer communistic practice and greater dependence upon and submission to Moscow.[2] Punishment for the Prague Spring was a defining feature of this program, and it took many forms.[3] The city of Bratislava was partially destroyed by the construction of the New Bridge across the Danube as one third of the historic district was bulldozed to pave the way to the flats in Petržalka. But what impinged even more on people's consciousness, and therefore on their range of expression, were not the most dramatic exercises of totalitarian power but the least. As Václav Havel has described, the communist regime in Czechoslovakia succeeded in repressing people not primarily by killing them—that would create a "story" and thus a motive for uprising—but by subjecting their every move to a "network of bureaucratic limitations." According to Havel, if citizens wanted to travel, change jobs, or engage in any program of study, they would face the stifling bureaucratic regulation of their everyday choices:

> He is usually compelled to undertake a long and exhausting march through various offices for the necessary permits, certificates, recommendations, and he must frequently demean himself or bite his tongue. It is tiring, boring, and debilitating. Many people, out of disgust, or for fear it will drag them down, quickly give up on their most personal plans. In doing so, they renounce something of their own potential story. . . . Culture and information controlled from the center narrow the horizon against which people mature. The demand for unquestioning loyalty forces people to become bit players in empty rituals. People cease to be autonomous and self-confident participants in the life of the community and become instruments with which the central agent fulfills itself. The ever present danger of being punished for any original expression compels one to move cautiously across the quicksand of one's potential, a pointlessly exhausting process.[4]

Although the phrase "network of bureaucratic limitations" did not arise verbatim in the narratives of my interlocutors, each one of them could with varying degrees of ease recognize the particular restrictions to which Havel speaks; all the manifestations of the network Havel describes, together with their deleterious effects, appeared in their narratives of learning and using English under the "normalized" communist regime. The central control of information, the demand for loyalty, the empty rituals, and the danger of punishment all left their imprint on people's encounters with English. At the same time, however, English was not to be made a "story": it was not to be completely banned, overtly discouraged, or otherwise "killed"—just hobbled. Because Soviet doctrine mandated English's containment, just as it did any other feature of the capitalist West, efforts to study the language, use it, or capitalize on its value were undermined, but not in any way that seemed deliberate or dramatic. Centralized mechanisms, including restricting the numbers of English classes taught and English teachers trained, quietly limited the number of students who could learn English in schools. Even though student demand for English outstripped that for any other foreign language, the regime would not allow that demand to be met; rather, it would do what it could to centrally control the number of English language speakers in the country.[5] These limitations on English were legitimated by a circular logic consistent with Soviet doctrine that articulated utility to the socialist state as one of its defining principles and separation from the capitalist West as another: English was not useful; therefore, it should be contained.[6] Because it was contained, it was not useful—though the notion of "utility" animated in this logic was quite artificial.

English was relatively less useful, for example, because every student "needed" to study Russian from primary school through high school (this requirement a blatant act of linguistic imperialism if ever there was one). Further, it was due to the regime's own machinations that the average Czechoslovak citizen was presented few opportunities to use English in life. Bookstores did carry some English books, but they were almost prohibitively expensive. The university library in Bratislava had a collection of English books, but because it was not openly shelved, but rather only available through request, its accessibility was largely limited to specialists. One could buy a British newspaper from the newsstand, but it would likely be the *Daily Worker.* There were no English language TV stations. Foreign films shown either on television or in the cinema during the 1980s were generally dubbed. American agencies were not permitted to give presentations of American books, and British presentations were limited.[7]

English education in the schools was designed to accommodate the general containment of English. English textbooks produced by the state during this period were overtly ideological. Lessons deriding the class structures of capitalist Britain and America seemed designed to discourage travel to these countries even if one could otherwise undertake it, but in most cases, one could not. If there was no "need" for most people to travel to the West, no pressing "need" to learn how to decode spoken English, there was no need for much instruction in conversational English. Apart from three British nationals employed in the 1980s at three different universities in Slovakia, who helped in teacher training, exposure to first-language speakers at the primary and secondary instructional levels was exceedingly rare. Instead students could devote their time to translation of nearly unspeakable passages celebrating striking workers, collective farming, and the egalitarian ideal of communism. The logic governing instruction in English in the schools was thus hermetic: English was to be presented in ways sharply disassociated from its growing uses in the world, because those growing uses signaled the unassimilable fact of the increasing vitality of global capitalism.

All four people I spoke with who appear in this chapter recounted the effects that restrictions on travel, broadcasting, publication, and ideological expression had on their pre-1989 efforts to learn English. Their stories of English demonstrate the subtle and yet nearly irresistible force with which the network of bureaucratic limitations impinged not only on the process of learning English but also on attempts to trade on its growing global value. The reader will note that the individuals profiled in this chapter are quite critical of the former communist regime. This does not mean these same individuals don't also have robust critiques of the West, and such responses are featured in later chapters. I found that among the people I interviewed, however, critiques of capitalism never led to a desire to have the old system back—not lock, stock, and barrel, at any rate. In the current Western academic climate, in which Marxism forms the springboard for many critiques of global capitalism, it may quixotically be the critiques of communism in this chapter that fail to resonate with Western academic audiences.[8] Unfortunately, the most forceful critiques of communism have historically been marshalled in the West by the extreme right wing; not only are these critiques leaden, but they provide very little analytical vocabulary for understanding communism in practice. That vocabulary, this chapter finds, is best provided by those who have lived through it.

The vignettes presented here collectively add an important chapter to the history of the global spread of English—a history thus far dominated by accounts of the impact of Western colonial powers on their satellites past and present. For the people who grew up under communism, English was shaped most by Soviet imperialism and the government's desire to maintain the illusion of communist self-sufficiency. As their accounts attest, however, the communist regime was far from self-sufficient; it suffered particularly from a lack of technically significant and commercially viable information. English was in fact useful to the communist regime, still invested in keeping up with the West's advancements in technology and trade—areas in which the Soviet Union and its satellites were, by the late 1970s, decidedly falling behind. These uses of English were, as much as possible, deliberately undervalued, as the official orthodoxy painted the West as backward. English was marked as the language of capitalism, a lingua non grata, literally a language undeserving of recognition.

IMPERIOUS VANITY

I begin then with the seeming—but only seeming—embodiment of imperious vanity and self-recognition: Jan, the corporate lawyer with several BMWs. For a short time as a young child, Jan spoke English more fluently than Slovak. In late 1967 Jan and his family departed for England, soon to be followed by many others who left Czechoslovakia for points West during the Prague Spring of 1968—the country's great experiment with political liberalization. Although the main reason for the move was to allow Jan's father, a pediatric surgeon, to work on a grant, another purpose was to introduce the children to English. Jan recalls that his parents were so determined that the children learn English that they did not speak to them in Slovak the whole time they were there; Jan and his sister and brother were separated in school by design so they wouldn't even talk to each other in Slovak. In 1969, with the expiration of the grant looming, Jan's father had to choose whether to stay in England or to go back to what was then an occupied Czechoslovakia. Jan said of his father's decision to return, trying to explain what in retrospect might seem inconceivable, "If you would ask him about it now he would say it was a mistake, but who knew they were going to lock down the country for another twenty years?" He explained the choice was not so simple. They knew that if they failed to return, their extended family would be persecuted.

Once placed within the confines of "normalized" Czechoslovakia, Jan's parents struggled to continue their children's education in English in whatever authorized and semiauthorized ways they could. The family set up and enforced rules for using English in the house, for example, designating the top floor the "English speaking zone." This special division of the house into English speaking and non–English speaking areas enacted on a smaller scale the sharp spatial-linguistic divisions produced by Cold War borders. The family made a game of these divisions, trying to catch each other violating the house rules if they spoke the wrong language on the wrong floor. I am tempted to locate in such games the root of Jan's playful approach toward English, considering his interest in cockney rhyming slang, license plates such as "2 FAST 4 U," and the NATO phonetic alphabet. But as with cockney English, a language developed by London's underworld, Jan's family's English was intended in part to circumvent the dominant linguistic order. Jan explained: "During the communist regime, we were not sure. . . . Everyone thought that telephones were tapped and things like that, so we also spoke English on the telephones to make things a bit more difficult." To this day, Jan's family still speaks in English on the telephone. From this early training in information management, Jan became more fully schooled in the power of language; later, in the capitalist economy, he would hold business meetings in English if he wanted to throw off his native German speaking clients and keep the upper hand.

To continue the children's education in English, Jan's family had to use their social networks to counteract the corruption of the official channels of linguistic supply.[9] "With great difficulty," Jan stressed, his father was able to use his connections to arrange for friends from England to visit—representatives from pharmaceutical companies who could negotiate certain sales with the ministries. Jan's parents would take these representatives to their cottage on vacation so that for a while, Jan would be immersed in spoken English. Jan's father would also ask the representatives to bring plastic bags full of paperbacks when they came. Jan remembers reading Alfred Hitchcock stories and Alistair MacLean novels, all gifts from his father's English connections. He acknowledged: "They were not bringing political literature, because they knew it was sensitive. . . .When they were asked at the border they always said, 'They're my books. I'm reading them.'" Out of these books, Jan's father fashioned lessons in English, explaining to Jan that while languages have more words than you could ever learn, any one author only used a small subset of those words, repeated in different contexts. Rather than having Jan look up each word he didn't know in the dictionary, he instructed him to keep reading until he figured out the word's meaning in context. Without these books, Jan said, he would not have been able to progress beyond the child's vocabulary he had picked up in England.

Whenever he could, Jan's father used his connections to take the children out of school in Slovakia for a month to send them to school in England. The children were able to travel, without parents, to England for four short stays in the late 1970s and early 1980s, living with English families with children of similar age: "It wasn't possible for the whole family to travel at the same time because the secret police would think that you were about to emigrate." Jan credits the paperbacks and the trips entirely for his proficiency in English, maintaining that he never studied the language at all from a regular textbook. I was somewhat surprised, then, when he mentioned that his parents had enrolled him in one of the few primary schools in Bratislava with an English program and that he had studied English in Slovak schools for years, up through university. For Jan, this detail was all but irrelevant. His central point was not what English instruction was ostensibly provided to him by the Czechoslovak state, but how he was dissuaded from pursuing English through those very entities ostensibly charged with promoting it.

Jan considered his firsthand experience with "native" speakers of English an ironic deficit in his Slovak primary school. His teachers of English, he noted, were unable to speak "proper English," which in his estimation required extended exposure to native speakers or an Anglophone country. He remembers vexing one teacher who, as he put it, "couldn't cope" with having a student in the class with superior English ability. He rebelled against her disfavor by reading his paperbacks under the table but was eventually caught for not reading the textbook. What he regarded as the banality of the typical English textbook at the time would be his undoing: "The texts would be very stupid, like 'Mary met John and they go to a theater or something,' and she would ask me questions like 'Who met Mary at the railway station?' I wouldn't know of course because I wasn't preparing for the lessons. . . . And this was good enough for her to give me the worst note, because she had proved I was not studying."

Jan often mentioned to me that he possessed a refined sense of justice, a prerequisite for life as a lawyer. Accordingly, each anecdote in his narrative suggested that any sense of justice one might cherish in the nor-

> Odpovedzte podľa skutočnosti [Answer according to reality]:
>
> 1. Do you know the names of any streets in the West End? 2. Is the West End different from the East End? 3. Can London workers afford to live in the West End? 4. Who can afford to live in the West End? 5. Do rich people live in the East End? 6. Are there different classes of people in Britain? 7. Is it the same in Czechoslovakia? 8. What about Czechoslovakia before 1945?
>
> —Josef Pytelka, Anna Janská, and Karel Veselý, Angličtina Pre I,
>   Ročník Stredných Škôl

malized communist regime of Czechoslovakia would be challenged by an absurd bureaucracy. In Jan's primary school anecdote, the bureaucratic limitation on display was that Jan, at that point nearing fluency in English, had not only been placed in a class with beginners but had been expected to act like a beginner. He had tried to explain in English his sense of this injustice to his teacher: "I was explaining to her that it wasn't important that I wasn't studying the stupid text because I could speak English, unlike the others." No longer keeping his English ability under the table, he let English fly at his teacher and was nearly expelled.

Jan did not abandon his unpopular quest for recognition of his English ability after primary school. Two more anecdotes illustrate Jan's (and Havel's) contention that Czechoslovakia's regime valued the dominance of the Communist Party above law, morality, and intellectual plurality. In 1988 Jan sought a language certificate from "the" state language school—"there was only one," he underscored, noting the effect of the centralized economy on the sphere of language certification.[10] In part he sought this certificate because it carried the weight of a university degree, but he also saw in it a possible escape route: "Such a qualification could enable me to travel abroad, being employed in some communist foreign-trade company. It could just as well be the key to freedom, then. Certainly, this was also on my mind, as nobody knew that the regime will collapse so easily." Although he did not take classes at the school, and the test for the certificate was designed to follow the classes, "legally," he stressed, one could apply for the exam without ever taking any of the school's courses. He was discouraged from applying to take the test, however, by the director of the school, who asked Jan if he was trying to prove that the teachers were there just for nothing. Jan in turn insisted on taking the exam and passed. In Jan's reckoning, the director's unwillingness to sanction any knowledge of English the school didn't have a hand in molding spoke to the regime's investment in controlling the circulation of English. If Jan's read on this encounter is correct, his request had the effect of bringing to the surface widespread anxieties (alluded to by Havel) that one's professional position served no purpose; the mandate to be employed, no matter the job, often meant there would be little connection between one's training and/or desires and one's employment.

Jan had by 1988 nonetheless begun to make money with his English, supporting himself in part as a research assistant at the Slovak Academy of Sciences, where he wrote reviews of English legal books in Slovak and acted as an interpreter for foreign visitors whose international language was English. Here again he experienced a disparity between his legal rights, insofar as his work with English was concerned, and how he was treated. By Czechoslovak law he legally had "the right" to higher compensation because he was an interpreter and translator, but he was never given it. He said the director who denied him the extra money told him, "'By accepting this [compensation] you would have a higher salary than Mr. [X] Jr., for instance'—his father was a very important party . . . [pause] . . . party animal—'and we cannot do that. That's it.'" "Regardless of your ability," I offered. "Regardless of the law," Jan corrected, highlighting that level of mastery was not at issue here. What was at issue was the maintenance of the party's dominance in all areas.

Jan's conflict with the director demonstrates his attempt to exit the circular logic the regime employed to place English outside the laws of Czechoslovakia and the dictates of the global marketplace; Jan insisted on the tradable value of English within the world and within the law. It was clear to him that English had value—otherwise why would he be needed to summarize English legal works? Collectively Jan's tales of injustice outlined the features of English that were peculiar to the language's position within the "normalized" Czechoslovak state: nothing about what Jan was doing with English at that time was inherently political—reading paperbacks, being bored in class, asking to sit for exams and to receive salary raises to which he was entitled—but the place of English as a controlled language under communism made these actions affronts to what Havel called "the imperious vanity of the administrative apparatus," an apparatus that sought only to fulfill its own underlying ideology in practice. Jan's refusal to defer to this vanity in his efforts to acquire English both called into action the regime's constraints on intellectual plurality and questioned their legitimacy. But adding even greater insult, Jan highlighted the growing value of English in the world.

GENERAL NERVOUSNESS

I met Jan in 1994 through Peter and Alicia, a married couple I had known since 1992. Alicia in the early 1990s was perhaps more typical than Jan of Slovak speakers of English, in that she had studied the language for years in school but felt it difficult to speak, having had very little practice. By 2003, however, she had been presented with more than ample opportunity to practice. Thanks to her and her husband's ability to outbid (in other words, outwork) Western software developers, Peter and Alicia found themselves in their sixth year of living in the South of England, renting out the house they had left behind in Slovakia to Jan and his family. (Jan was building an exquisite house overlooking the Danube—possibly to rent out to foreign Volkswagen managers.)

When Alicia first moved to England, the spoken vocabulary she most sought focused not on the words of work, however, but on the words of motherhood. Not too long after the family had set up their home abroad, she emailed me a list of phrases in Slovak and asked me for the appropriate English translations. They were all phrases for managing the unruly British friends of her daughters. When we met in 2003 at a restaurant in suburban Bristol for one of our interviews, Alicia looked around with horror at what she had come to call "wild British children," squealing, coughing, running around "nearly naked." These children signified to her the social decay of the West. She sighed, "Communism was horrible, yes, but could we please keep just some things that were good?" On that particular evening, she meant child-rearing practices that held children in check, but she also acknowledged another side to her discomfort with the ruckus.[11] As we left the restaurant and headed back to their BMW (formerly Jan's BMW), we passed a group of British teenagers laughing and carousing.

She noted that her immediate reaction to this sort of public display of joy was that it was somehow wrong. She would never make noise in public like that or call attention to herself.

Alicia had learned the value of lying low through a life deeply affected by the overt acts of political resistance of her parents' and grandparents' generation. In 1968 Alicia's father, a member of the Communist Party, signed a memorandum protesting Russian influence in Czechoslovak society and outlining Slovak communists' expectations for the future. When the Russians shortly thereafter invaded, Alicia's father was kicked out of the party and frozen in place in his job as a mechanical engineer. If Jan's family's way of protesting the regime was tactical (indeed, their English was tactical—for example, used over the phone to hide what they were saying), Alicia's family, so visibly discredited, was successfully dissuaded from even subtle forms of resistance. Nothing about the memorandum and its aftermath was explicitly explained to Alicia, who was of necessity kept in the dark; had she spoken about her father's transgression at school she could have gotten her family in further trouble. Ignorant of the memorandum, she was nonetheless aware something was amiss: "He didn't tell us anything. It means we went through all our young age and we didn't understand properly what is communism. We understood only something is wrong there."

Alicia's father conveyed to me that his action had not been the only "škvrna" (taint) on the family. Her mother's uncle had immigrated to Canada in 1948 to avoid the political persecution meted out to those who fought with the British instead of the Red Army against Hitler. As punishment for the emigration, her mother's father was demoted from his job as a manager, and his land was seized. The repercussions of this punishment later reached Alicia's mother, who was not allowed to go to university and who promptly thereafter forgot the English she had studied in high school. Eventually the repercussions reached Alicia as well.

Initially, however, before Alicia "properly" understood communism and her family's place in the political order, she was motivated to learn English in the hopes she might someday communicate with her great uncle in Canada. While English was not offered at her primary school in the midsized city where she grew up, she elected to study it at *gymnázium* (college-preparatory secondary school) and ran home to tell her mother

---

The British and American Systems of Government

The most important office in the American system of government is that of the President, who is elected for four years. He is the head of the federal government and his powers are even wider than those of the British Prime Minister. But the President, whoever he is, never acts against the interests of Big Business, i.e. powerful capitalist groups, which control both the Republican Party and Democratic Party as well as most of the American press.

—Josef Pytelka, Anna Janská, and Karel Veselý, Angličtina Pre III, Ročník Stredných Škôl

---

of her choice. She was completely surprised when her mother, who had also chosen to study English in high school, declared her decision ridiculous, complaining, "Why have you chosen English? You should have chosen the French language." When Alicia asked why, her mother responded, "Because another brother is in France, and it's nearer!" In fact, this other brother, from Alicia's grandmother's side, had emigrated in the 1930s and subsequently dropped out of contact: no one had any intention of looking for him. Alicia's mother's ironic comment, therefore, conveyed less the potential usefulness of French and more the absolute pointlessness of learning English. You're not going anywhere, Alicia understood her mother to be saying. This argument would resonate in Alicia's mind throughout the years she studied English, as she became more and more aware she might never use the language.

It seems incongruous that Alicia was first attracted to English with the thought that she might speak it one day, because she considered having to speak a foreign language torture. Alicia thought that speaking a language might be easy for students "who wanted to be actors" or for other extroverts, but it was not easy for her. Halfway through her first year, she was barely passing. Alarmed by her grades, Alicia's parents engaged the services of a tutor, a colleague of her father's whose job at the plant was to translate technical materials coming from the West. Most of these extracurricular lessons were devoted to correcting what Alicia felt to be her worst problem: "I was shy to pronounce." She recalled enduring her lessons only to be hounded afterward at home by her grandfather, who tried repeatedly but unsuccessfully to engage her in English conversation. Retired by the age of sixty, her grandfather had finally been given permission to visit his brother in Canada, and he had begun to study English in preparation for his trips. (Alicia explained that once her grandfather had retired, he was no longer a worker for the state, but rather a burden and thus expendable. She pointed out with a smile, "If he would run away, no one would miss him because they would have to pay him [retirement] money.") According to Alicia, her grandfather would ask her questions in English, angling for a response, but Alicia would run away—again, shy. "He tried always to speak with me but I was refusing. I was shy to speak with him."

In Alicia's last years of high school, her class was one of two in the country selected for a pedagogical experiment that cut across the curriculum, thus including her English lessons. This experiment was, to Alicia's understanding, an attempt at Western pedagogy. Contrary to the Slovak system in which tests were given frequently, her class would only get tested at the end of the year. The course materials were different as well. Alicia noticed, for example, that she had different books than her friends—"thicker," and without so much "pure" communist ideology. But still, she maintained a disinclination to throw herself into learning English and an even greater disinclination to speak it. Even without explicit communist ideology in her textbook, she felt her English lessons nonetheless were shaped by the regime's bureaucratic limitations. None of the incentives Alicia might have been presented to study English seemed to counter the weight of her despair about communism's omnipotence, which she had absorbed from her parents; the more robust communism seemed, the less likely she imagined ever having a chance to use English. Although she herself had never experienced any overtly punitive aspect of the system, Alicia's "shyness"—her sense that speaking English would be calling undue attention to herself—remained an expression of her family's precarious relationship to the political system. I note the words she emphasized below, in her account of how her parents' despair and her growing perceptions of the limitations on her own mobility affected her motivation to learn English: "My parents were quite pessimistic and unhappy in communism. And this pessimism probably went on me. And I took it to myself as: *Why* will I have to study languages? It will never *fail,* this communism, I will never go out, and I will be *locked* here in this country. I'm not going to study. *Why?* What for? . . . My mom she was studying it for years. She never *used* it, and she never had the opportunity to use it. It was kind of, um, like, protest in my body. I refused to study because I was very unhappy locked there in the country. Even I haven't understood in this time so much what's going on, yes, but I *felt* this lock in my country. I cannot go *there* and it bothers me." To the outside world, Alicia's rejection of English would only be apparent in poor marks. But for her, this rejection was something internal, "in her body," a protest against being locked in a country with no genuine reason to use English. Her repeated stress on the word "why" illustrates how fruitless the pursuit of English seemed. As Havel suggests, this feeling of pointlessness and its accompanying tendency toward self-censorship are products of a climate in which politically motivated reprisals are routine. Investments made in Alicia's English—whether by her school, her grandfather, or even her parents—were undermined by the larger political climate, which created, as Havel has suggested, "a state of general nervousness: no one is ever sure of the ground he stands on, or what he may venture to do, or what he may not, or what may happen to him if he does."[12] Her parents had internalized this nervousness and, in turn, passed it on to Alicia, who absorbed it with every tutor's lesson and every state test. What she did not absorb quite so completely, however, was English.

UNQUESTIONING LOYALTY

Alicia's husband, Peter, was like Alicia the inheritor of punishments for a genealogy of infractions against the communist state. In 1968, Peter's father, Milan, a physicist, was enjoying a summer of agricultural work and touring in England. Milan tried to convince his wife to bring their two boys to join him for a more extended stay, but Peter's mother didn't want to leave Czechoslovakia, her career as a pediatrician, or her extended family. Milan accordingly drove back from England, entering Czechoslovakia on August 20, 1968. "I drove over one border," he recounted in 2003, motioning with one finger over the table where we sat toward an imaginary East. "The Russians drove over the other border." The finger of his other hand headed "West." He smiled cheerily when his fingers met. "Next morning I woke up, tanks everywhere." I had heard a less cheery version of this story from Peter's mother when I visited them in their modest flat in Bratislava in 1992: "He was very angry," she said of her wanting to stay in the country. She looked over her shoulder at her husband who was walking toward the kitchen and added as an aside, "He's still angry."

Although Milan had returned in 1968, his sister, unfortunately for Milan's family, had not. She had also left Czechoslovakia for what she imagined to be a temporary trip with her husband as he pursued a degree in West Germany. The Russians invaded, and she never did return, largely because she and her husband might have faced a jail term upon reentry. Nevertheless, punishment for her infringement was visited upon her relatives, and it was multigenerational in scope. Peter's grandfather lost his job as a high-ranking minister of foreign trade and was sent from Prague to Bratislava to become a teacher of economics and foreign trade. Milan lost his professorship at the Slovak Academy of Sciences and was demoted to the lowest rank of instructor at the technical university, where he was permitted to teach though he was barred from giving examinations. The education of his two sons, both toddlers in 1968, would in time be curtailed as well.

Peter's family's degradation or something similar, in all likelihood, would have been visited upon Jan's extended family had Jan's father failed to return to Slovakia in 1968. Peter's parents were certainly similar to Jan's—doctors and scientists who knew English and used their reading knowledge of it to keep up with advances in their professions. Both families placed a high value on cosmopolitanism and found folk nationalism unappealing. Here, the scene of my 2003 talk with Peter's father has significance. Our interview took place at a restaurant in Hungary at Hegyeshalom, a town on the border between Austria and Slovakia. Nested in a highway oasis, the restaurant joined a gaudy but down-market casino, a truck stop, and a highway hotel. Although self-consciously Hungarian themed in its menu and decor—thousands of dried paprika pods hanging in bunches from the ceiling—the restaurant took currency from all surrounding countries. Conversations at adjoining tables took place in a blur of languages, making the restaurant seem a Central European never-never land. Peter's father was no stranger to such a mélange: married to a Czech, he had grown up in the part of Slovakia that had by 2003 been given to the Ukraine.

Peter shared his father's cosmopolitanism. When I asked Peter why he had learned English and why he felt it was important that his own daughters learn English, he called on an old Slovak proverb: "The more languages you know, the more human you are." Peter, a humanist, saw in the proverb an invitation to learn languages to improve one's soul and character. But his invocation of the proverb in the context of our interview—as a rationale for his daughters' learning English rather than, say, Swahili or some other less economically strategic language—suggested a certain repurposing of an old expression to fit the imperatives of the postcommunist terrain. He was not alone in making such gestures. The Commission for the European Communities of the EU adopted the proverb as the epigraph for its 2005 communication on the subject of multilingualism.[13] The commission, however, stretched the sense of the proverb somewhat in its recommendations, which included calls for the European Union to develop multilingualism via the promotion of computer translation programs—hardly a step that would lead to people learning more languages and one that might potentially cut down on the need for human translators.[14]

Although Peter equated being "human" with depth of soul and character, his personal history made accessible yet another meaning of "human" pertinent to learning English during communism: that is, in the eyes of the regime, Peter's English made him more human because it made him more flawed, more liable to corruption and error. It was through English that Peter became more vulnerable to the regime's dehumanizing tendencies because his knowledge of it would show his failure to fulfill the regime's demand for unquestioning loyalty.

Peter's sense that English could be a liability began early. His parents chose to send him and his brother to a primary school and later a *gymnázium* specializing in languages just so they could learn English. ("German, they could learn from television," Peter's father remarked with a shrug.) On the surface, Peter enjoyed an unusually rich English education: he had English books that were all in English, with no portion in Slovak or Czech, and a language lab complete with BBC tapes. He noticed, however, that his Russian teachers were actually Russian, whereas his English teachers were Slovak. Later he began to understand that the school's reputation for preparing Russian translators helped compensate for the shortcoming of also specializing in English. As he progressed to the *gym-*

názium, Peter became aware that his teachers were regarded as members of the intelligentsia and were therefore watched: "Because they were doing English, they were not very popular with the party. There were educated people there. . . . They were trying to teach us more and be open."

According to Peter, the "natural" trajectory from this education would have been to go on to a university to study law or medicine or to get a philosophical doctorate; these paths would have entailed further study of English to some degree. He was particularly interested in becoming a doctor, like his mother; however, the reverberations of his aunt's emigration fifteen years before interrupted his plans. When I asked why he couldn't follow his dream and his mother's example by attending medical school at Charles University, he replied, "Communism. . . . We were on the blacklist, so we couldn't go to such universities." His parents had advised him and his brother not to apply to any medical program, because at that time one could only apply to one place once a year, and they would have almost certainly been denied. If denied, Peter explained, "You could lay bricks somewhere for one year, try again, with a very clear result apparent to anyone"—in other words, certain rejection. His father was able to first check unofficially with his technical university to make sure his sons would not be applying in vain.

Peter described the study of English in his technical university as "just reading technical stuff," though in all other ways it was similar to the level at which he had been taught in primary school. He was also at that point exposed to English through software and hardware manuals (he and Alicia bought an Atari computer together). Meanwhile he pursued the human aspects of language learning outside of school. He formed a band playing Beatles songs, which he loved. With Alicia, he put together a tape of English expressions so Alicia's grandfather could study for his trips to Canada. What was most humanistic about this gesture was its attempt to aid the recovery of what had been lost during "normalization": the family. If emigration and the ensuing punishments marked one of communism's most inhumane aspects, English, if used to bring people back together, acquired in opposition a humanitarian valence. The language could be a bridge to the taboo West, as well as a potential medium to reunite a family rent apart.

By the time Peter entered mandatory military service in 1989, he had

---

Lesson 22: On a Co-operative Farm

13 April 1969

Dear Ruth,

This time I am sending you some snaps from a co-operative farm. In one of your letters you asked me about our work there. Well, it is like this: We go to the farm on Fridays. We mostly help with vegetables, but some six months ago we also helped with fruit. In winter, or also when it rained, we worked in the farmhouse. . . .

—Josef Pytelka, Anna Janská, and Karel Veselý, Angličtina Pre I, Ročník Stredných Škôl

---

been well schooled by the regime as to his various culpabilities. Assigned to a secret camp in the Czech part of Czechoslovakia, a little farther from Alicia—by then his wife—than he wanted to be, he attempted to get himself transferred by playing up his knowledge of English as a further liability.[15] Unfortunately, his efforts went horribly awry. Peter, who had inherited every ounce of his father's talent for relating horrible events while grinning from ear to ear, described his meeting with his superiors on the second day in camp: "They found out that we have a quite, let's say, smart guy here for the subject [missiles], but politically he is unbearable. He shouldn't be here. What are we going to do?" Peter told the secret agent present at the meeting all about his aunt, but since "they knew obviously everything already," he felt he needed to embellish the story here and there to appear an even greater security risk. He had never had any contact with his aunt whatsoever, not even a letter, but when they asked him directly if he had any communication with her, he replied, "*Lively* contacts." They asked if he knew this was a top-secret camp, and he replied, "Of course, and I don't think I should be here." Then they asked what languages he used to communicate with his aunt's family, and he told them German and English. "And nothing was true. I just wanted to get out and be nearer to Alicia. That was the only reason."

English, one might note, need not have entered Peter's narrative here at all. His aunt was in Western Germany; certainly the lie that they communicated in German would have been sufficient, but Peter was at this point trying to rhetorically mobilize the volatility around English as the language used for very little else besides communication with the West. That his plan backfired badly suggests that Peter, while appreciating the subversive value of claiming to communicate abroad fluently in English, had also severely underestimated its impact on his superiors' perception of his allegiances. After the meeting, they restricted Peter's physical movements as much as possible. Rather than transfer him closer to Bratislava, they kept him within the camp to perform menial and unpleasant tasks, including conducting alarms at all hours of the night. They denied him any holiday or leave to go see Alicia or his parents. "I was the black sheep there. . . . It means you cannot do nothing till end of this service. You won't go anywhere, you say something you go to the prison one, two, seven days . . . and those days will be added to the end of your service." As Havel has described, one of the goals of the communist regime's punishments was to shrink the space in which one could act. Peter had tried to mobilize English to expand that space, but because the language was threatening unless the regime strictly controlled its use, the space around him shrunk further. Fortunately for him, the year was 1989. While he was at camp, the Velvet Revolution occurred, and the "normalized" state of Czechoslovakia came to an end.

BITTEN TONGUES

I would like to depart from the extended clan of Peter, Alicia, and Jan to introduce Fero, a person whose history demonstrates that even if one had never run afoul of the regime, the network of bureaucratic limitations would nonetheless impinge upon one's relationship to English. Fero grew up in Brezno, a city long considered a gateway to the more industrial Eastern Slovakia. His family did not engage in any open defiance of the communist system that he acknowledged. When his mother was threatened with losing her teaching job if she failed to sign a document in 1969 saying she agreed with the Soviet invasion, she, like thousands of others, no doubt most of them also with bitten tongues, signed it. His father was an electrician who did not know English, unlike the fathers of Jan and Peter. No one in his family had ever traveled to the West, much less emigrated.

During our 2003 interviews, Fero, by then a university instructor of British and American history, continually historicized his experience

> The date of May 1st was selected as the result of events that had taken place in Chicago on May 1st. At that time big strikes were being held in the U.S. with the aim of attaining an eight-hour working day. The Chicago demonstration was scattered by the police. Six persons were killed. The trade unions called a protest meeting for May 4th. The peaceful demonstration was upset by several agent provocateurs who threw a bomb at the police detachment. The police retaliated, brutally arresting the leaders of the workers.
>
> —Till Gottheinerová and Sergej Tryml, *A Handbook of English Conversation*

under communism as if to say that there was nothing singular about his life. He spoke, for instance, of the communist ideology pervading English textbooks in his school in terms of "we": "They must have been adopted to suit our socialist needs, as it were. We had these articles about these workers, and we were fed these images of workers in the Western world but the topics are similar. . . . So even if people learned English before 1989, they had to do it through topics such as Worker's Union in the West and that kind of thing." These books presented the communist construction of "real" lives, the lives of people who worked in factories and didn't dally with cultural or intellectual pursuits, but rather devoted themselves to undoing class privilege.

Fero first encountered such texts at the age of ten, when his mother put him in an English language program in primary school. Like Jan, he felt that the poor nature of the instruction he received was due to the teacher's lack of contact with native speakers: "In those days, there were not many people who spoke English, and those who did, did not have any contact, so I wouldn't blame her for that." He would have liked to continue his education in English in secondary school, but that opportunity was not forthcoming. He wound up, as he put it, "bored" in a vocational school designed to churn out electricians, where English instruction was tentatively offered for one year and thereafter just "disappeared." Because he was at a vocational school, he explained, languages were not considered useful.

Fero's mention that he had gone to vocational school came as something of a shock to me. When I met him in 2003, he was pursuing a Ph.D., the highest educational degree of anyone I interviewed, including those who had attended college-preparatory *gymnáziá*. When I asked how he had wound up at the lowest rung of secondary education available during communism, he delivered a narrative filled with pauses and gaps; he seemed to struggle to define the agent who had sent him to become an electrician, eventually deciding it must have been himself: "Well, I was trained to become an electrician because I wasn't . . . [long pause] . . . I remember, perhaps I wasn't a very good pupil, although perhaps my marks would not tell you that, but I was an average student, so I didn't get to the secondary school that I wanted to, a *gymnázium*—that would be the flagship of secondary schools; if you want to go to university you go to a *gymnázium*—but because I was not clever enough I went to vocational school. . . . And because I studied at a vocational and technical secondary school, I was only allowed to go to a technical university. I wasn't able to get this recommendation for humanities, for example." At this point in the interview, Zlatica, Fero's wife, who had been listening in from a spot on the floor of their one-room "flatlet" (as Fero termed it), glared at her husband and grabbed her hair with both hands. The moment the interview was "over," Zlatica challenged Fero's account of his educational history. Considering that some years after the Velvet Revolution, Fero was accepted to graduate study at Cambridge University on the basis of a thesis he had written on phonetics, it is difficult to credit as anything other than sarcasm his assertion that he went to a vocational school because he wasn't "clever enough." Fero countered, "It's quite fashionable nowadays to say 'I was a victim of communism,' but the fact is I failed the test." Zlatica responded, "But you *were* a victim of communism." According to Zlatica, the test was beside the point. Given the regime's practice of funneling even unwilling students into technical schools, Fero, she believed, had never really been given the option to go to *gymnázium* in the first place.[16] Technical schools and vocational programs had indeed proliferated during communism, and some form of technical or vocational education had become the most expected course for students after primary school, particularly male students. Fero's sister, Zlatica pointed out, had not been as trapped as Fero because she was female.[17]

When Zlatica rejected Fero's narrative of his path to vocational school, she rejected with it his narrow definition of victimization. She had a broader view of victimization, one that encompassed limitations on what to read, what to do, and where to go. She saw what Havel would define as the "anonymous administrative apparatus" in the regime's privileging of a certain version of utility—doing something with one's hands—over other forms of work that Fero might have enjoyed or been suited for. Zlatica's account of victimization would include the lack of decent materials Fero had for developing his love of English on his own. It would include as well a system through which someone would be tracked unwillingly into a vocational school and then would be kept from higher education, particularly higher education in the humanities, unless the extraordinary intervention of a recommendation, rarely available to those outside certain sociopolitical networks, was granted. Had Fero tried to gain such a recommendation, he would have become embroiled in one of those bureaucratic adventures Havel describes as "demeaning." Unsurprisingly, Fero had not even pursued it; the result of his efforts would have been all too predictable.

Zlatica's vision of communist education as an administrative apparatus feeding uninterested students into technical education is substantiated by documentation from the period. Placements were made not on the basis of grades or performance alone but by a "special commission" that could produce a rather nuanced account of a student's talents and propensities. Attempts to sway students toward an interest in technical education, however, began much earlier in a student's life than the eventual decision by special commission. Primary school students were encouraged to acquire technological hobbies and read technical magazines. Students in rural areas were introduced to mechanized agricultural production. Despite (or perhaps because of) these efforts, the number of applicants for technical higher education was considered chronically below quota, even into the 1980s, when Fero would have been a student.[18] Given that such mechanisms existed to increase enrollments in technical schools both at the higher and the secondary levels, and given as well that many of my interlocutors who were teachers during this period reported rampant corruption in the admissions system, I now believe that either Fero did not fail the math admissions test or the test was designed to be unreasonably difficult in order to ensure a strict cap on the number of *gymnázium* students, weeding out those applicants who might have been more inclined toward the humanities. Although there is no way to confirm what happened in Fero's case, I think Zlatica's perception of Fero's situation is accurate: he never really had the choice to go to *gymnázium* in the first place.

It was clear to me that, although this part of Fero's past was painful for him to recount, he viewed the inevitable renunciation of his personal plans as an unnoteworthy sacrifice compared to others demanded by the communist regime. Once, when he and I discussed the relationship between McCarthyism in the United States and communism in Eastern Europe, he remarked, while acknowledging the injustice of Americans being sent to prison, "The difference is, here, you'd have been sent to a uranium mine." Because Fero was always conscious of the uranium mine as a possible fate, being tracked into vocational schooling did not rise to a comparable level of victimization. This is, however, precisely Havel's point: the uranium mine was the quintessential story of totalitarian oppression, the worst case of bad cases. It was, in Havel's terms, "a story." Yet as Havel contends, the communist regime was most effective at repression when it did not create such stories but rather stifled people's will to pursue even modest ambitions.

Zlatica's comments thus tried to make a story out of what Fero was insisting was no story. Her insights laid out the logic of the communist regime's containment of English—a containment that operated without having to present itself in the form of outright repression. Vocational schools were not censoring English. They were simply focused on developing skills with immediate practical application, and English had little widely perceived practical application. In the Czechoslovak pedagogical system of the time, based as it was on Marxist-Leninist dialectical materialism, curricula were developed explicitly to marry theory and action.[19] Students were to have the opportunity to practice production in factories, mines, and farms. Because English was rarely used in such domestic industrial and agricultural sites of production, the language appeared to occupy the realm of theory rather than praxis. The regime could nevertheless maintain such an appearance only by denying the growing global story of both the knowledge economy and English.

"PERHAPS IT IS TIME . . ."

The network that was the Soviet Union collapsed between 1989 and 1991, as Michael Hardt and Antonio Negri have aptly observed, largely under the weight of its own internal contradictions.[20] Certainly one of these contradictions emerged in the treatment of English. Hidden between the lines of the narratives of my interlocutors, in which English seems to have been without a real-world use, are instances in which it obviously was necessary, even during the communist regime. English allowed communication with other countries in an increasingly global economy and enabled access to critical technical information. English appears in this capacity in Jan's account of being a translator for the science faculty and in his certainty that knowing English could have gotten him a job in "some communist foreign-trade company." It appears in Alicia's account of her tutor's day job: translating technical materials from the West into Slovak. The highly qualified nature of Alicia's account of her tutor's work at the factory, however, demonstrates that such uses of English, while necessary, were fraught: "She was translating the technical stuff that was coming from West. . . . They were always catching up with the newest technology—trying. It was communism, yes, but they needed the translation. Also translating back because they were producing, and they were also cooperating with the West, not only the East. Not so much, but they were." Lastly, English emerges in Peter's account of working for a foreign-trade firm before military service. This firm traded with other countries for fuel, Peter told me, and much of its business was conducted in English.

When English was critical to a certain technical or commercial mission, it had value in communist Czechoslovakia, but that value was not broadcasted widely or even, in the case of Jan's experience of being a translator, acknowledged in terms of economic exchange. English was thus denied full recognition of its fast-approaching status as the global lingua franca. Russian was the only lingua franca acknowledged in a state where Soviet doctrine maintained the fiction that the USSR and its satellites comprised a self-sufficient entity. Keeping English out of circulation in this way gave it a certain character: desirable in some ways because it was elusive; intimate because it could potentially restore one's contacts with departed family members seemingly never to return; undesirable too because nothing, ostensibly, could be done with it. However, it remained in all cases inextricably linked to an imaginary of capitalism that would in time prove to be a bit different from the real thing.

The containment of English during "normalization"—what Alicia called "pure communistic time"—in the Slovak part of Czechoslovakia could not have been sustained without the omnipresent threat of Soviet intervention. The effects of this threat were perhaps thrown into sharpest relief by what people opted to do after 1989, when it was in abeyance. Peter did not return from military service to his job as a database developer at the foreign-trade firm. No longer under the regime's mandate to be employed, he elected to be unemployed for six months to study English full-time with a native speaker. Fero, who after 1989 decided "Perhaps it is time to do something that I would enjoy," quit technical university, and, no longer needing a recommendation, applied to university to study English language and history. He became one of the first Slovaks to travel to Britain after restrictions were lifted. Later, he participated in boiling a Slovak-English dictionary that neglected to give examples of word usage in real-life contexts.

But perhaps the best "story" is that of Jan, who just before the Velvet Revolution figured out how to use the network of bureaucratic limitations together with English's growing global worth to his own advantage. He devised a plan to import and sell personal computers—almost unheard-of luxuries in Slovakia at that time—from Austria. He knew full well, of course, that importation for the purposes of resale was illegal, even given reforms the regime had instituted in a last-ditch effort to sustain itself.[21] To get around this restriction, Jan applied to open a Slovak-English translation business so he could have a legitimate reason to get the computers into the country. Filling out the paperwork to start the venture, he told the woman behind the counter that his parents were forcing him against his will to start the business and asked if she would please reject the application. While the application was under consideration, he made a day trip to Austria, upon his return handing the border guard the necessary paperwork to allow the import of the computers he had purchased. At home his application to start the translation service was rejected in short order by the sympathetic clerk. He explained to me that at that point, according to the law, "I had no choice. I had to sell the computers." He took the money and bought—what else?—his first car.

2

Other Worlds in Other Words

The unified Czechoslovakia emerging from the Velvet Revolution of 1989 did not last long. In January 1993, the country officially split into the Czech and Slovak Republics in what has since been widely termed "the Velvet Divorce." Such a term acknowledges that compared with the violent and traumatic rending of the Balkan states, the breakup of Czechoslovakia was relatively peaceful, resulting in no deaths. Although not necessarily a primary cause of the split, nationalism certainly followed the split in Slovakia; in this respect, developments in Slovakia paralleled those in many other postcommunist states in the 1990s, even those that did not experience a redefinition of nation-state identity. As anthropologist Katherine Verdery has observed, visible ethnonationalism in these states was supported by diverse groups sharing one thing in common: they did not envision an easy place for themselves in the market-driven order of the future.[1]

Language politics in Slovakia carried much of the burden of articulating ethnonationalism in the immediate postcommunist years. Although

Slovak had been the de facto official language of Slovakia, as early as 1990 the Slovak Parliament passed legislation to assert that all official documents must be published in Slovak. The Slovak Constitution, ratified two years later, even more explicitly recognized Slovak as the official language of the state. Vladimír Mečiar, the populist yet internationally unpopular prime minister of Slovakia who presided over the creation of the new nation-state, ushered through the passage of the 1995 Law on the State of Language, which enacted sweeping limitations on the use of minority languages. Communication in virtually all spheres of public life—education, the judiciary, the media, health—now legally had to be conducted in Slovak. The obvious goal of this legislation was to disenfranchise Slovakia's nearly six hundred thousand ethnic Hungarian citizens;[2] Mečiar's government oversaw the removal of bilingual road signs in ethnic Hungarian-dominated towns in the south of the country, challenged the existence of public schools in which the language of instruction had historically been Hungarian, and encouraged the spelling of Hungarian names in phonetic Slovak.[3]

In such a period of strong ethnolinguistic and nationalistic identification in Slovakia, how are we to understand the simultaneous but seemingly incongruous growing appetite for English? Almost overnight after the Velvet Revolution, schoolchildren in both ethnic Hungarian and ethnic Slovak towns stopped learning Russian and starting learning English. Ethnic Hungarian and Slovak adults alike enrolled in English courses. The project of macroacquisition of English in Slovakia proceeded uninterrupted by the language laws declaring Slovak the official language of the new nation, the appeal of English irrepressible or, at the very least, nonthreatening to the nationalists.[4]

It might be tempting to read these years as a mere changing of the guard, when English, the language of Western imperialism, simply replaced Russian, the language of Soviet imperialism. This view recognizes a real shift in continental power relations but nonetheless fails to explain what Slovaks wanted from English and what forms of available English they gravitated toward.[5] It doesn't explain, for example, the local and personal concerns that led two Slovaks, whose stories form the heart of this chapter, to embrace two nationally marked varieties of English. Here we rejoin Fero, the aspiring student of English who sought to perfect pronunciation of Britain's most highbrow dialect—Received Pronunciation—as a counterstatement to both the nationalism of Mečiar's Slovakia and the socialist teachings of the past. This chapter also introduces Maria, an aspiring artist and an aspiring master of colloquial American English, who imagines far-off America as a "Dreamland" of "many people, many theatres," during a time of cultural crackdowns in her home country. While the Slovak Republic was going through its crises of national identity, Fero's and Maria's adoptions of English constituted attempts to bring forth alternative social arrangements to the unsatisfactory political situation that surrounded them.

To the extent that these two individuals had always wanted to learn variants of English of which they had little firsthand knowledge, from countries they had not even seen until the 1990s, they were chasing imaginaries of English. These imaginaries would in fact prove awkwardly mismatched to their circumstances when Fero did manage to get to the United Kingdom, initially as an agricultural laborer and subsequently as a participant in a workshop for teachers, and Maria did manage to get to America, as an art student and then as a starving artist. But the Englishes in which they had invested so much time, energy, and indeed dreaming did at least initially provide them a distinct, individual identity to set against the homogenizing strains of populist nationalism in Slovakia's early years as a new nation. When I asked Fero why he wanted to master Received Pronunciation, the dialect he called "the model for kings and queens," he explained: "It has to do with my personality. . . . I've always felt more comfortable being in the minority rather than the majority, and the majority of people when they start learning English in Slovakia, they tend to have an American accent. It's easier for them." As Fero's comment suggests, although British English was widely taught in schools as the standard, the typical English language learner in Slovakia tended to speak with something closer to an American accent.[6] Fero considered his command of the "posh" dialect of England an accomplishment that set him apart from other Slovaks, including those he worried had adopted a disastrously anti-European stance. Maria similarly looked to American idiomatic English to distinguish herself as an "international" artist at a time of nationalist cultural retrenchment and stretched resources for the arts. She saw the language of American popular culture as the key to the art world outside Slovakia's border.

Fero's and Maria's initial imaginaries of English, however cosmopolitan, were nonetheless entirely enabled by the relative isolation of Slovakia from the West during much of the 1990s. By 1997, Slovakia had fallen well behind its immediate neighbors on the accession track to the European Union, in no small part due to the government's treatment of the Hungarian minority. It was not until the 1998 replacement of Mečiar as prime minister by the far more free-market-oriented Mikuláš Dzurinda that the country would seek a place in the EU in earnest and through that process become enmeshed in the forces of globalization it had hitherto kept at arm's reach.[7] As Slovakia moved toward capitalist integration, it moved as well toward embracing English as the medium through which profit could be generated. At this point it became clear to Fero and Maria that their national Englishes had become anachronisms. As market forces began to dictate the place and form of English in their respective professions, Fero and Maria, instead of feeling themselves empowered, began to speak of English in terms of complexities: what it did for them, what it couldn't do for them, and in some ways what it did to them. Their knowledge of English was no longer the knowledge that counted. As they moved between Slovakia and England or Slovakia and America, they felt they had less grasp of the language, not more. In the midst of Slovakia's entrée into an EU whose raison d'être was ostensibly the freer movement of goods, services, currencies, and people, Fero's and Maria's own movements became circumscribed, and the resources that had fed their English fascinations became scarcer, their favored institutions, broadcasts, and books casualties of an economy that saw little value in their steady linguistic devotions.

LETTERS TO AMERICA

I have a photo of Maria taken in my class in 1992. She's wearing a tee shirt a friend made for her depicting John Lennon in his post-Beatles, political agitator, New York years, her own hairstyle a mirror of Lennon's. She's leaning over the guitar she's strumming to read from a notebook in which she has written the words to a Simon and Garfunkel song. I remember this moment vividly. One student had copied the lyrics from her book onto the blackboard with the meticulous handwriting that all the students then seemed to possess, and the whole class had joined Maria in singing: "I'd rather be a sparrow than a snaaaaail . . ." "El Condor Pasa" was the one piece of American popular culture that we, the teachers, had not ourselves introduced, and it had for that reason a strong claim on the students' attention. They gathered around Maria as they sang.

I remember I felt grateful for this moment of relative amity in the class during what had been an otherwise dicey two weeks. Ethnic Slovak and Hungarian students, who spent most of the year learning in their respective native languages in their respective schools, had come together to learn English in our intensive two-week course—but they'd only come together physically. From morning till midafternoon, they sat together in the classroom but often refused to work with one another. Their dictionaries had become symbols of their mother-tongue identification; the ethnic Hungarian students had initially kept theirs in their desks, out of view of the majority Slovak crowd. Only occasionally did open hostilities flare: one Hungarian student complained to me that when she interviewed her classmate for one of our conversation exercises, her classmate had responded to the question of what she liked and disliked, "I don't like Hungarians." There was nothing inherent about English, or the exercise of being schooled together, in other words, that would release political tensions then rife within the country, though Simon and Garfunkel for a moment came close.

It was fitting that Maria had brought the song that had briefly pulled everyone together: she was one of our more cosmopolitan students, for reasons both geographic and familial. Maria grew up at the confluence of the Morava and the Danube rivers, which forms the southwestern border of Slovakia. As a child she had played in the ancient sand dunes above the rivers, a spot that gave her ample opportunity to peer at forbidden Austria from behind the guard towers erected along on the riverbank. She grew up in a house of artists: her mother edited an art magazine, and her father was the financial director of a renowned and widely traveled folk dance troupe in Slovakia, one of the few cultural organizations showcased internationally by the country. A public figure in Slovakia in 2003, Maria's father had a view of the commercial heart of Bratislava from his spacious and beautifully furnished office. His walls displayed international awards and framed "thank you" letters from places where the troupe had performed, including one from the mayor of a town in New Jersey that Maria's father, not knowing English, could not himself read. Both of Maria's parents managed to sustain careers in the arts without knowing English, but Maria knew that she could not. Increasingly, she served as language broker for her family, translating letters written in English for her father that requested the troupe's appearance abroad. English, to her, was associated with the arts, and the arts, for Maria, would be more and more associated with America.

American popular culture, Maria attested, was the reason she had chosen to study English beginning with her first year at *gymnázium*. The Velvet Revolution occurred in the middle of that first year of secondary school, bringing with it dramatic changes to the English instruction she received. No longer would English be taught as a dead language; instead it would be the language students might actually need to speak. Maria described the abrupt shift: "So the first half [year] we had communistic books of English that were bad. . . . They were made just like the Russian, just an article with dictionary and a little bit of grammar. It was not a speaking language." But after the Velvet Revolution those books were replaced with "the *real* books of language, the *real* manuals of foreign language. . . . I think they were imported." She emphasized the word "real" in her descriptions of the new textbooks, her further comments unpacking what she meant: These books had pictures. They had empty lines beckoning the students to write within their pages. They didn't have any Slovak in them or any communist ideology. They would ask her to speak. But perhaps most crucially, to Maria, they came from the country whose language she was studying. They were thus artifacts of another place, a "real" place, and that aspect, more than the actual content of the instruction, seemed to appeal to her.

Maria had an American teacher of English at her disposal beginning in her junior year of high school. She remembers that this teacher wasn't particularly well trained, but she also remembers she didn't care. The key thing to her was that this woman was foreign. Maria's desire to meet even more foreigners drove her to take the summer course where we met. It was her choice, not her parents'. She enrolled, she said, "because we didn't really have a lot of chances to meet foreign people still even in 1992." Maria distinguished herself from her fellow students by maximizing her exposure to my fellow teacher and me, the resident Americans. She took every field trip offered by the course, even one to Devín Castle, nearly in her backyard. But perhaps most telling of her commitments was the fact that she kept up a correspondence with me for years after 1992. These letters consistently identified America as an artistic and cultural hot spot—that much was plain to me at the time I received them. It was only in retrospect, however, looking at the letters collectively, that I noticed they shared a generic pattern: some personal information about her life, followed by a generally dour political update, followed by a seemingly unrelated and considerably more upbeat review of an American movie. For Maria these movies seemed no less "real" than the political situation around her, which she considered so absurd as to be surreal; like the textbooks she encountered in *gymnázium,* the movies actually came from another place, one she imagined hopefully as quite unlike the place where she awaited them.

Maria first wrote me in December 1992, four months after the close of our summer course. She described her plans to apply to universities in drama and fine arts but then discussed the impending splintering of the country: "I disagree with this because I have many friends in Bohemia and think everything (or majority) is better there (schools, theatres, actors, movies, shops . . .)." At the end of this lament, Maria asked if I had seen *Little Man Tate,* a movie she had just seen. For Maria, Czechoslovakia's split into the Czech and Slovak Republics moved her one step further from her connection to culture; *Little Man Tate* was what remained. The movie was also the piece of life that she and I potentially shared.

In February 2003, shortly after the split, Maria sent a somber letter on the subject of the pomp of nationalism and her distaste of it: "My letter comes to you already from 2 months old independent Slovakia. 31st of Dec. we had big celebrations in all state. Big fireworks, anthems sounded from every radio stations, many drunkards and skinheads in the streets . . . etc. . . . I celebrated nothing. Our first man of government (Mečiar) is taking off all other politicians. I think in our state it will soon be 'rule of one man' or 'absolutistic monarchy.' Grrrr." After mourning the end of her country, she described the America of her imagination, a country, unlike the newborn Slovakia, almost hyperbolically shot through with art and culture from end to end: "Big land, many people, many theatres, cine-mas, concerts, nice nature. . . . We have three theatres, five cinemas, big air pollution, one good school, one good concert. . . . When I will have some-times money and possibility I must see your 'Dreamland.' I'm very curi-ous. Really." The juxtaposition of the political degradation (in her view) of Slovakia and the imagined cultural ascendancy of American culture was, interestingly, not parallel; America to her never seemed a political utopia, but a cultural one.

A couple of months later, in April 1993, Maria wrote of the impact of the unstable political situation on Slovak schools: "We have (finally) our president" (here she sketched a picture of a man on a stamp with the parenthetical comment "he is fat"). "Constitution not yet. High prices, low salaries. There are no money for schools here. They have to finish the school year earlier in some schools." She noted with chagrin that some people wanted communism back and commented only, "Horrible." This letter continued with movie reviews of *Toys* and *Bram Stoker's Dracula.* She finished with a flourish: "Please write back and when you'll meet on the street Robert De Niro or Barbara Streisand or I don't know . . . give them my regards please." The America of this letter was still somewhat hyper-bolic and dreamlike, with stars roaming the streets (of course she was be-ing facetious here), but this would mark the last time she spoke of America as a far-off imaginary place she might reach "sometime." Her project to get to America quickly became more pragmatic.

In 1994, after a short period in which he was temporarily unseated, Mečiar regained his position as prime minister. Maria's letter captured the moment in both word and image. She commented that Mečiar had won the election and added with sarcasm, "but, of course, we're getting better!" She mentioned that a friend of hers from the United States had observed that no one smiled in Slovakia: "I was a little surprised. I thought that there was no other funny state but Slovakia. . . . I've been convinced that we were state of comedians and all of them are in government!" She drew clowns in the margins.

In this letter Maria included along with her movie reference (*Forrest Gump*) several exercises in American idiomatic expression. She wrote: "I know some new American Sayings so I start with one of them: It's colder than a witch's tit." She had just begun her study at the Slovak Academy of Fine Arts and described herself as "busier than one-legged man at ass-kicking contest." Later in the letter she threw in a third colloquial phrase: "I'm still planning to go to study to America but it doesn't seem very hopeful. Probably I won't gain the scholarship but 'Rome wasn't built in a day.'" Not only was she plotting her physical escape to America, she was spending a good deal of time invoking America through its vernacular. The letter itself was doubtless practice on a more basic level for Maria. At one point she wrote, "I'm fresh and ful of vigour" but "vigour" appeared above the scribbled-out "ardour," suggesting that none of these letters was written without some effort (and that she often deferred in matters of spelling, as almost all Slovaks did, to the British standard taught in schools). Nevertheless, she seemed far more concerned with accumulating colloquial English expressions than with grammatical standardization.

It was with Mečiar's third government, formed in 1994, that Slovak politics took a turn toward the surreal. In 1995, President Michael Kovač's son was abducted, knocked out, and dropped across the border in front of a police station in Hainburg, Austria. Because Michael Kovač Jr. had been wanted for questioning in Germany in relation to fraud charges, it was widely believed that the secret service under Mečiar had orchestrated the abduction as revenge against the president, his political enemy. Shortly thereafter, the contact person for the key witness in the investigation of the abduction was killed when his car exploded. These events caused international and domestic alarm, but Mečiar's coalition continued to exert even greater control over the media and the political process.

Maria did not mention the kidnapping in her letters, but she did remark on the new Slovak language law that had made Slovak the official language of the new country: "By the way, there's new law here. 'Law for protection of the republic.' If you say anything against the republic or government in public place you can be arrested. And another law. Law for Protection of Language. Slovak language (of course). It means, if you say anything what's not in proper language at public place (if you are public person) you have to pay. Well Mečiar:"

At this point Maria abandoned words completely, ending her statement with a drawing. A cowboy, right out of Maria's Hollywood "Dreamland" of America, put an end to the creator of her nightmare of national devolution:

FIG. 1. Assassination of Mečiar. Drawing by Maria Corejova.

Maria next wrote to me on October 10, 1996, concerning an invigo-
rated crackdown on culture and the arts under the Mečiar regime. When
Minister of Culture Ivan Hudec closed theaters and installed regime loyal-
ists as directors to promulgate a "Slovak" program in the arts, thousands
of people took to the streets or signed petitions to "save culture."[8] Maria
documented this: "There are new demonstrations here against the minister of culture. There are political fights in theatres, thousands of people
are on the squares shouting. It's *very* similar to something from before 6
years." She mentioned incidentally that she had gone to see *Jesus Christ Su-
perstar* in Prague and, although expecting a bad copy of the American play
(as she knew it from the American movie), had been pleasantly surprised.

Maria's trips to the movies and to plays apparently provided more
than an unconstructive escape from a disappointing and distressing political situation. Going to pop-culture movies functioned in tandem with
her critiques of the cultural changes in the new Slovak Republic. Maria,
who had grown up under a communist regime, with its mandate that art
should serve the state, and come of age during a nationalist resurgence,
with the continuing mandate that art should serve the state, certainly
found Hollywood movies escapist, but not in an apolitical or aesthetically

naive way. Maria was in fact concerned with the aesthetic limits of nationalist art. In a follow-up interview with me, she declared the offerings exhibited in galleries before 1989 "soc-realist pieces of crap." With the culture wars of the early Slovak state as a backdrop, Maria's consumption of American pop culture and American colloquial English clarified the need for even "useless" art, in all its forms. She was not so much escaping her own world for another, but constituting an imagined world for herself, one larger than the locally celebrated but to her problematic vision of a self-sufficient and West-renouncing Slovakia.

In 1997, just as support for Mečiar's regime was crumbling under international pressure, Maria's life became dramatically affected by international currents. She met a German lesbian in Slovakia and realized for the first time that she herself was gay—or, better put, she realized that "lesbian" was a possible, if difficult, identity she could adopt. To survive in rigorously heteronormative Slovakia, Maria sought out gay and lesbian organizations that themselves drew largely on international models and languages to establish their viability.[9] She also made her first visit to America as an exchange student and began to develop an understanding of the economics of the global art scene; this understanding, however, marked the beginning of the end of her love affair with colloquial American English.

THE ARTIST WHO DOESN'T SPEAK ENGLISH

The line that most resonated from my interviews with Maria was, "The artist who doesn't speak English is no artist." The global dominance of English in the marketplace meant that English and the production and recognition of art had become nearly one. While Maria developed into an artist consummately interested in universal problems of translation of experiences (i.e., how one person can feel, see, hear what another feels, sees, hears), she became over time increasingly frustrated that she was compelled to render her statements through translation into English. By 2003, "the artist who doesn't speak English is no artist" (a line she had picked up, ironically enough, from a Western art magazine) perfectly conveyed her situation.

Initially, English was absent from her artwork. In 1999, when Maria and a fellow student from the academy of fine arts first explored translation as a universal problem, they were concerned only with the act of translation between language and experience. Their first project started when one of the pair left a note in Slovak for the other, asking her to draw a particular dream. Maria and her collaborator conducted a series of these exchanges and subsequently exhibited the handwritten letters and the pictures together. They soon realized, however, that this project couldn't be exhibited outside of Slovakia or the Czech Republic, because no one would understand it; one final act of translation—that between viewer and work—would remain elusive.[10] They faced, at once, a language problem and an artistic problem.

Maria thereafter considered English essential to even the most modest form of international exposure. When she and her collaborator moved to video as a medium, they continued their exploration of translating one person's reality into another person's art, but they adapted their work for eventual display in Hungary and other Eastern European countries. Maria translated the audio of the video into English subtitles so the work would be legible to the largest portion of the international audience they aspired to attract. The majority of onlookers would thus undertake yet another act of translation, translating from the global language of the arts—English—into their own language. Maria explained that the subtitles were something of a compromise. Her preference would have been to render artworks entirely in Slovak because, she said, "It's my language and I cannot really express what I want in English—of course because it's not my language—but if I do it in Slovak, I definitely have to put subtitles there because language is important and it's important that people understand it. And when I want to have international people to understand it, I have to make it in English." The "having to" bothered Maria. The purpose of her art was to allow one person to share ontologically an experience with another, with art as the only mediation. The introduction of English, an idiom with which she was not completely comfortable, created exactly the kind of distance it was the point of her art to collapse. Inevitably, English moved even closer to the core of her projects once she began producing work in America, collaborating with Americans. In these videos, all the dialogue would be in English, and Maria's American interlocutors would do ever more of the talking; Maria, in later projects, was mute.

English had, of course, always been embedded in the means of production of Maria's artistic process. She had encountered it in her tools of the trade, in software manuals, textbooks, and other supplies produced in America. Her planned doctoral thesis was a translation from English into Slovak of theoretical/critical texts on new media art. The art school periodically paid her to teach other students how to write a CV and talk about their work in English. Her entire professional existence, in other words, revolved around bringing the cultural linguistic norms of the Western art world to Slovakia and communicating the value of the artistic products of Slovakia to the West. At a certain point, English not only made her art legible but became her art, which is why the statement she had stumbled upon, that "the artist who doesn't speak English is no artist," hit so close to home. Concurrently, and wrenchingly, she discovered through her trips to America that knowledge of English (plus her talent) would be necessary but not sufficient to secure her a place in the international art realm.

In the spring of 2003, I visited Maria in Boston, on an unseasonably cold and wet weekend. In her apartment that she could no longer afford to heat, I interviewed her for this book. When we began the interview, Maria and I were both soaked and freezing, having walked twenty minutes through the rain from the train station after waiting in vain for a bus that had failed to make its scheduled appearance. In that setting, "the artist who doesn't speak English is no artist" became particularly redolent. Maria delivered a disquisition on the geopolitics of art at the advent of the twenty-first century: "These days everything is going on mostly in U.S. and mostly New York. All art scene is there, and it seems like when you want to be somebody in the art world you have to live in New York and you have to be there. . . . When you look at the art magazines, they're talking only about either American or Western artists and no Eastern artists. They just don't exist. . . . I think this artist was from former Yugoslavia, and he meant it that way: 'The artist who doesn't speak English is no artist.' It means when you are not there, you aren't anywhere." What did it mean for Maria to not be "anywhere"? It meant to be where she was: in freezing cold Boston, as close to New York as she could manage to come, courtesy of an American grant that had fallen far short of imagining the needs of Eastern Europeans with no savings in one of the most expensive cities in the United States. Even with her extra work as a home health aide, the expenses of the city overwhelmed her; simultaneously, the resources of the school she had mistakenly chosen to affiliate with underwhelmed her.

As a result of having underestimated the costs of heating and everything else, sometimes she and her Slovak partner, Mona, who had joined her for the year, ate only a potato for dinner. Since I had last seen them when they visited me in Illinois six months before, she and Mona had become perilously thin, and Mona had developed red lines under her eyes and a persistent cough. During my visit to Boston, Mona produced some gold coins and asked me if there was any place she could sell them. They were desperate for money to pay back a loan Mona's father had made them. Maria had invested a lot of years and a lot of study of English in her dream of becoming an artist in America. But by the exceptionally chilly and rainy spring of 2003 when we met in Boston, she had given up. Although she had spent the first period of her fellowship trying to figure out how she and Mona could stay in America permanently, she said she couldn't wait to go back to Slovakia so she could feel "human" again.

During this period Maria also shifted her artistic focus to consider how she might reveal, rather than fight, her conflicted feelings toward English. She designed a project whereby an American friend in a distant location (in this case me, in Illinois) would speak words in English that she would write in Slovak on a table in Boston. Maria conveyed these directions to me in an email: "Think of some words in advance which describe your feelings or notions of distance. I picked up this topic because we were so estranged (good expression?) for so many years, there is a distance between us right now . . . and there is language distance in terms of understanding." After so many years of writing to one another, there it was. We were estranged. Writing in English created, rather than collapsed, the distance between us. Maria had given up imagining English as the way to connect with me and with America absolutely and had begun instead to use English to highlight its insufficiencies as a medium of communication.

Another evocative phrase from my 2003 interviews with Maria was "because I love America"; she used it several times: to explain, for example, why she had chosen to study English in high school and why she had come to America on three occasions to study art and, indeed, just as a general statement about herself. Each time, however, she signaled sarcasm, by either a forced smile followed by a cascading laugh or mock fervor in her voice and eyes. When I checked back with her about this sarcasm in a later email, she responded by summing up the changes in her attitude about English: "It was freedom back in 1989 because you didn't have to do it but you could. And it was symbol of western world which meant freedom. Now it's a little somewhere else. You still don't have to learn it but on the other hand you have to again if you want to stay compatible with the world of 21st century . . . unfortunately or thank God? We cannot speak about freedom again. It's a kind of new slavery, which is of course different from the previous one." In the end, Maria's plan to live as a New York artist would be undercut significantly by American restrictions on immigration, plus simple supply/demand issues in the American arts: too many artists, not enough demand for art. After a year of starving in Boston and a memorably depressing visit to a Czech friend living in a basement in Harlem, she decided that if she planned to be an artist she was going to be poor, and it was much better to be poor in Slovakia than in New York City. The lack of a viable public sphere in the "Dreamland" of America scandalized Maria and Mona, who were forever editorializing: "We thought your roads would be better." "We thought your buses would be better." They were mystified by the economics of how these public works could be much more developed in Slovakia (a far poorer country) but in the end found their answer through American pop culture, in an episode of *The Simpsons* they saw in the United States.

Homer Simpson, Maria related to me, had been fired from his job in the nuclear power plant. When someone suggested to Homer that he become a bus driver, he, incredulous at the very thought, responded: "A bus driver?!? Only Blacks and lesbians ride the bus!" This was a revelatory moment for Maria, explaining the crucial flaw in her project. All that America was ready and willing to grant her, a Slovak lesbian, was the distinction of being marked for inferior public transport. The dystopic vision of the United States offered by *The Simpsons* had clarified the gap between her "Dreamworld" of the past and what she experienced in the present. The day after she related Homer's dilemma to me, we were back on the bus, heading from Arlington into Boston, sitting silently in our freezing wet misery after again having waited twenty minutes in the rain. Maria looked around at our fellow passengers, virtually all African American women, and turned to make a comment to me—in Slovak: "Len černoši a lesby chodia autobusom" (Only Blacks and lesbians ride the bus). She said this with exaggerated slowness, mimicking the drudgery of the bus.

By 2003, in the midst of her stay in Boston, the colloquialisms of American speech had become slightly less charming to Maria. Her final analysis of the phrase "the artist who doesn't speak English is no artist" was a definition of how the world works: "It's true, because all the world speaks English, and all artwork speaks English, so if you don't speak English you can't catch up. Catch up? Catch on? Whatever." There was a time when Maria would have put some effort into trying to nail down that colloquialism, but no longer. She used English—indeed, needed it—much too much to sustain herself in a realm where American colloquialisms held little immediately transferable capital. Her perfectly timed "whatever" nevertheless captured more of the naturalness of American colloquial speech than she had ever possessed before, indicating that she had triumphed at least in arriving at some reality of global cynicism and ennui.

LINGUA CLASSICUS

Like Maria, Fero was appalled by the nationalism he saw blossoming after the split up of Czechoslovakia. Taking the international view, that it represented a step Eastward, backward, and toward a different kind of restrictive isolation than Slovakia had suffered under the communist regime, he called Slovakia's experiment with self-direction in the 1990s "a disaster." By late 2003 he was looking forward hopefully to the country's expected accession into the European Union the following spring. He feared what would occur should Slovakia fail to join forces with what he felt were the more established democracies of the continent. It is in the context of this fear that I read his pursuit of his favored brand of English: Received Pronunciation. Fero admired British government and culture and reveled in their embodiment in Slovakia in the form of the British Council and BBC broadcasts. He repeatedly acted to preserve the influence of these entities in Slovakia, viewing them as keys to maintaining not only his own English but also Slovakia's connection to the world.

Recall that Fero was so passionate about English that he once boiled a dictionary he considered a distortion of the language. I happened to be carrying an edition of the offending text on one occasion when we met. He saw it in my hands and declared immediately: "That's a terrible dictionary. In fact, we boiled that dictionary." His main objection was that the dictionary gave no examples of English as actual "native" speakers used it; it only provided one-to-one translations of Slovak words into English. For Fero, such one-to-one translation provided no avenue into the world of the British speaker. Languages and worlds were mutually constituting in his view, and his chosen English gave him another environment to inhabit. He embraced Received Pronunciation because it distinguished him from many Slovaks, who, he felt, spoke with more of an American accent. He told me he "always felt more comfortable being in the minority rather than the majority." As a mother-tongue Slovak speaker, he was, in fact, otherwise very much in the linguistic majority in Slovakia, but Fero strongly identified with Slovakia's minorities and sympathized with them in the 1990s, when they were politically envisioned to be interlopers in the new Slovak nation.[11] He told me that one of the most difficult aspects of his work as an examiner for the Cambridge certificates was that a few of the questions he had to ask served as invitations for some students to express their ethnonationalism. For example, he said, a question asking an examinee to describe his town might result in the answer, "I don't like my town because it has a lot of Hungarians or gypsies in it." Fero found it difficult to do what he had been taught he must as a Cambridge examiner: sit there with a straight face so as not to affect the outcome of an objective test of English ability. Such moments were an unwelcome intrusion into the English Fero relied on to create a comfortable space free of postrevolution ethnonationalism. His attachment to Received Pronunciation, otherwise known as "the Queen's English," equally suggested a rejection of the communist past. Certainly, if one had hated communism as much as Fero did (and he truly, deeply hated communism), one could do little more to articulate that hatred than master the most highbrow dialect of Marx's object lesson of capitalism's failures: England.

I had often wondered where Fero had acquired his fascination with England; his desire to learn British English predated the significant influence of British (or even American) cultural organizations in the country, so it was not the outcome of any successful neocolonial action. The British Council, England's embodiment of the English language teaching industry, had a minimal presence in Slovakia until 1992. By that time Fero had already been to England several times. I realized long after my interview with Fero, however, that the communist regime he had lived through was itself the metatext that kept England ever present in a Czechoslovakia walled off from the West. Karl Marx, writing *Das Kapital* from London, had decried England as the "locus classicus" of the capitalist mode of production.[12] Fero had been attracted to England specifically because it was the recognized antithesis of socialism. He thus studied the Queen's English as a lingua classicus: the most resonant linguistic symbol of that world. He began to achieve his greatest proficiency, however, just at the time English was proliferating rapidly into world Englishes, becoming unmoored from its traditional national and cultural associations as it spread across the globe and specifically through Slovakia. The potential loss of those associations disturbed Fero. They were what he had wanted most from English. What was the Queen's English without the Queen?

"I WAS REALLY CLOSE"

Fero's desire—every bit strong as Maria's—was to *get there,* to find a way to live in the land of his English. After the Velvet Revolution, he became one of the first postcommunist Slovaks to visit the locus classicus both of England's capitalism and of Received Pronunciation: the South of England. In the summer of 1990, he and a friend, pursuing a tip from a newspaper, paid a fifty-pound fee to apply for agricultural work in England. Fero thus became part of an itinerant labor pool the British, at least initially, actively courted.[13] He didn't learn much English, however, from his Eastern European bunkmates on the farm, nor did he witness much mainstream English life, save for his relationship with his employers. When I interviewed him in 2003, he still recalled with fondness a farmer he had worked for in the North, who was, he asserted (surprising me), "a socialist," unlike the "capitalist" farmers of the South: "He paid very good wages, and he was a very nice man. . . . He must have been one of those utopian socialists because he really cared about the people who worked on his farms. He talked to them. The farmers in the South of England that I've worked for were typical representatives of capitalism. They were polite, but they would not hesitate to wake us up very early in the morning. . . . But we knew what we were in for, and we worked very hard. We did not complain." Interestingly, Fero found socialism in the Northern UK admirable, whereas he seemed to find it threatening on his own soil. Despite his kind words about the Northern English farmer, Fero remained steadfast in his quest to master the dialect of Southern England.

Fero's early trips to Britain provided limited opportunities to converse with actual speakers of English, thus helping him little toward his goal. For him, British Council office openings in Slovakia were far more significant for his linguistic development. Nothing "on an organized basis," Fero felt, existed to support English education in his country before the British Council. He had compensated for the lack of English instruction in his vocational school by studying one of the few English language textbooks available at the time, *Angličtina pre Samoukov* (English for Autodidacts), by Ludmila Kollmannová. The book disappointed him, though, because it failed to detail the specifics of dialect and pronunciation that Fero desired to learn. The British Council, however, provided materials not only on English language learning and pronunciation but also on English history and culture. Most important, however, the British Council brought native British English speakers to Slovakia, allowing Fero to gradually refine his pursuit of Received Pronunciation by modeling his speech after the speech patterns of others. After studying phonetics for his master's degree, he became even more selective about his accent. He told me he remembered clearly the moment he noticed that his favorite teacher—once again, from the North of England—deviated from Received Pronunciation in his articulation of the word *fast*. Fero carefully elected to avoid copying such speech patterns, staying on course to perfect the dialect of the South.

Hoping to live among the native speakers of his chosen English as something more than inexpensive labor, Fero applied and was accepted to a graduate program in linguistics at Cambridge University. He could not in the end enter the program because he could not afford the tuition. The memory of having to decline the offer to study at Cambridge still pained Fero in 2003. "I was really close," he said repeatedly, describing his acceptance to one of Europe's oldest universities as his greatest success. "That would have been wonderful," he sighed. Instead of the extended stay studying in Britain he had hoped for, Fero was only able to make one last short trip in 1998, this time to take a teacher's professional-development course at a university in Portsmouth. For him the whole point of the three-week trip was "to travel to Britain," albeit, significantly, not as a low-wage worker. Because everything had been paid in advance by the organization sponsoring him, and he had been sent for the purposes of study, "suddenly I felt more respect for myself," he commented. He reveled in Portsmouth's historic atmosphere, particularly appreciating Admiral Nelson's ship *The Victory,* in drydock there. Fero remarked that he did not sustain correspondence with anyone he had ever met in Britain—indeed, in our interview, he didn't dwell on any relationships with Britons beyond his employers—but his encounters with British tradition and history, those things he had before only read about in books, remained vibrant for him in 2003.

The year of Fero's study trip to Britain, 1998, marked the end of Mečiar's tenure as prime minister and the beginning of the end of Slovakia's estrangement from European and trans-Atlantic organizations. The previous year, Slovakia's isolation from the West had reached a peak when NATO issued entry invitations to Slovakia's three closest neighbors—the Czech Republic, Poland, and Hungary—but excluded Slovakia. A week later, invitations to negotiate European Union accession were issued to these same three neighbors, but Slovakia was again pointedly excluded, ostensibly for its failure to meet the EU's "democratic criteria," including passage of a law protecting minority languages.[14] Slovakia's economic woes, including mounting debt, made the country's indifference to Western transnational agencies difficult to maintain. Global economic pressures won out, producing a shift in Slovakia's political direction.

Beginning in 1998, under Prime Minister Dzurinda, Slovakia made swift strides up the EU accession track. Dzurinda reopened the investigation of the infamous Kováč abduction of 1995. Efforts were made to address linguistic discrimination against Hungarians in schools. Slovakia began to craft a reputation as a potentially dependable democratic state in international eyes—yet apparently not dependable enough. Late in 1998 Britain introduced a visa requirement for Slovak visitors, ostensibly to thwart Slovak Romany asylum seekers from entering the country. This requirement was kept in place until December 2003. Fero did not make it back to England after 1998. With his trip to Portsmouth, his engagement with England had reached its apogee, and Fero was left with pursuing Received Pronunciation only from afar.

"ALL THOSE YEARS AND ALL THAT ENERGY"

Paradoxically, the more Slovakia moved toward establishing economic and political norms like those of Great Britain, the harder it became for Fero to pursue his ur-British English. This situation frustrated and disappointed him. Due to the visa restriction, he could not easily travel to Britain, even as a low-wage laborer. Perhaps even more galling from his perspective, the British Council in Slovakia had begun pulling up stakes and moving to newer, untapped markets in other countries. He had relied on the British Council as a repository not only of English language teaching methodology and materials but also as some kind of link to the world that England represented for him, one of stability and democracy. In 2003, he rued several British Council office closings in the Slovak and Czech Republics, even as he saw those closings as a possible sign of Slovakia's political development: "I've heard that in the Czech Republic, most of the British Councils are closed, and I heard the only one is in Prague, so we're lucky to still have some here. But if that's a sign that democracy is still fledgling in our country, I don't know. But I don't know if I would be more happy to have a poor democracy and more British Council offices here, or a fully developed democracy and no British Council: I'm joking!"

To Fero's further disappointment, those British Council offices that remained in Slovakia had changed, switching their focus away from educational support and toward more marketable Englishes. His local British Council office no longer maintained a language teaching consultant position. The British nationals whose accents he had emulated had all gone. Fewer and fewer books on the humanities written in English were passed from the British Council to the library of Fero's university. Fero explained: "I think the British Council changed its philosophy . . . promoting business and that kind of thing. What I regret is that the BC [British Council] used to promote teaching more, and used to provide teaching materials for people, . . . and they used to have more British nationals assessing speaking."

Despite his misgivings about the British Council's new policy of replacing British assessors of speech with Slovak nationals, Fero himself applied for the job. He acknowledged a dual economic and personal motive underlying his acceptance of the position: "It is good money. But I've always wanted to do something for the British Council." Fero by 2003 made all his money through his English ability, in one way or another. Chiefly he joined the English Department faculty of the university in central Slovakia where he had gotten his degree. As with Maria, English had become completely integral to how he made his living at the same time as it was becoming more and more integral to Slovakia's place in the global market generally. Rather than seeming like a happy coincidence, however, this timing had made his relationship to English fraught.

Fero found himself buffeted by various forces new and old; fresh free-market pressures and entrenched academic practices conspired to make his position at the university paralytic. He taught fifteen English classes a week, while trying to pursue a doctoral degree in the "spare time" that schedule afforded him. He had originally wanted to study British history but found grants and fellowships from Britain for foreigners hard to come by and specialists of Britain within Slovakia from whom he could learn scarce. He soon transferred his intellectual interests to America to take advantage of the greater availability of foreign grants and spent one year in the Midwest (the same year Maria spent in Boston—on the same American fellowship) researching the United States' political interest in Slovakia during World War II. He found this dissertation topic uncomfortably distant from the topics that needed to be covered in the broad surveys of British and American history he was required to teach: "As academics, we should be teaching what we research, but the problem is that we can't really research what we teach, and some people at the top are not willing to recognize this."

Fero further thought it problematic that English was spreading within Slovakia while Slovaks were largely without the means to study England, the place whence, in his view, the language came. The university did not, however, share his opinion that studying English necessitated studying British history. Quite the contrary: "those at the top," as Fero dubbed them, continually wanted the faculty of the English Department to adjust their teaching to address market pressures attendant to English's preeminence in politics and commerce. There was talk of introducing a preprofessional major that would generate in-demand translators and interpreters. Fero's argument for keeping his department's focus on preparing teachers rather than translators highlighted necessity rather than marketability:

"There is still need for teachers of English. . . . We feel that we are producing people that are really needed." Fero acknowledged, however, that his department faced "external pressure to be more flexible in terms of the market." People wanted to make money with English, not spend their lives passing it on. Schoolteacher positions were not very lucrative and thus not very attractive to the most qualified; anyone with the energy to acquire fluency in English could make much more money working for the private sector. Even as the members of Fero's department resisted changing their mission, they faced competition from within their own university; a new English Department opened up with a philosophical rather than teaching faculty: "We are sort of threatened by competition, but we believe that we've been doing this for years, preparing teachers, and we believe that we're good at it, and we believe that traditions should be kept."

Perhaps the sign of market pressures most unwelcome to Fero was that the BBC in English, the living repository of the tradition of Received Pronunciation, was beginning to disappear from the dial. Fero had for years listened to the BBC World Service every morning, ritually. When he heard in 2001 that the BBC station serving central Slovakia might no longer broadcast, he sprang into action, amassing support for the BBC's continuance. He recalled, "I organized this petition . . . to be sent to the BBC to complain, because they left it [the BBC] in Bratislava." He argued that for educational reasons, and considering the pending accession to the European Union, the local BBC station should remain on the air. The petition proved unsuccessful, and the BBC in English was cancelled in his region in 2002. Fero, always just scraping by on the equivalent of the few hundred dollars a month that his position as a faculty member at the university afforded him (a salary supplemented with his work conducting Cambridge exams and requalifying former Russian teachers to teach English), bought himself a digital satellite so he could get the BBC World Service radio broadcast, plus BBC World. With this equipment and a VCR, he was able to tape everything he felt of value for classroom use.

Fero, in short, did his best to counteract the market pressures bearing on English so he could preserve the English he felt most significant for Slovakia's future. As a replacement for the British nationals who used to teach the language exams, and as a rebroadcaster of BBC material in Received Pronunciation for educational purposes, Fero had turned himself into a repository of Received Pronunciation. Yet by 2003 he had stalled out on his plan to go to England, much as Maria had stalled out on her plan to live in New York. The position he had adopted was, like Maria's eventual place in the Slovak art scene, a highly localized one in the global economy: one can't successfully be an Eastern European repository of Received Pronunciation in England any more than one can be a starving Eastern European artist in New York. These are the ruthless truths about locality that make a lie of the neoliberal rhetoric of the free movement of people, goods, and services. Fero's position exacted a great price on his personal quest for English fluency. He had by 2003 given up (again) in a small way on his personal plans, relinquishing his struggle to perfect the English of his choosing, an English that held value in his eyes not because it had the greatest purchase in the market but because of the history of his own efforts to acquire it through three regime changes in Slovakia: "My English is fairly good sometimes, but I've got—I make lots of mistakes, for example, when I try to use it in everyday life, talking to people like yourself, or talking about things that you do on a regular basis, because that's the area where I've got the most weaknesses, because I don't practice my language naturally. I use it for academic purposes. And that's really disappointing and disheartening because after all those years and after all that energy I've devoted to studying English, that's the area in which there are still weaknesses and they're not going to improve."

3   "We Live and Learn"

In 2001, the malls came to Slovakia: first "Polus City Center," just west of downtown, then the sprawling "Aupark Bratislava Shopping Center," incongruously abutting Petržalka's many Soviet-built cement-panel apartment buildings. Before I returned to Slovakia in 2003, after a nine-year absence, Maria gave me this advance notice on the malls: "Really, if you are inside one of these malls, you will not be able to tell where you are, in Slovakia, or in America." With this comment Maria enunciated a common observation about the working of globalization: that certain features of the American commercial landscape replicate themselves in many countries, seemingly with little regard for local features. Certainly part of the confusion of place Maria alluded to resulted from the generous use of English in both malls. In Polus, for example, corridors were labeled after famous streets of the West: "5th Avenue," "Regent Street." Such uses of English enabled local businesses to appear at least fictively as players in the global economy. That Polus had a corridor dubbed "Wall Street," for example, allowed the Slovak bank VUB to advertise on billboards that it could be found in Polus "na [on] Wall Street."

In 2003 I went to Polus to meet Goran, a manager of a biotechnical firm and an old friend. As we walked through Polus, Goran recalled that he had first seen such a thing as a mall in 1999, when he visited America on business. Hoping to find a present for a friend back in Slovakia, he shopped at an upscale mall in the suburbs of Washington, D.C., emerging stunned both by its expanse and by the expense of the items it contained. Goran mused, as we walked together down Polus's 5th Avenue, that it wasn't long after his return from D.C. that malls began appearing in Bratislava.

Goran directed me toward a bookstore to find what we were looking for, a current version of his favorite English book, *Angličtina pre Samoukov* (English for Autodidacts), by Ludmila Kollmannová. Goran had used this book to study English on his own when, as a teenager, he had had no opportunity to study English formally. Everyone knows this book, he told me; it was the only book of its kind during the communist regime. Indeed, numerous people I interviewed who had begun studying English before the Velvet Revolution did know it. This was the book that Fero studied on his own when no English was offered at his technical secondary school: "A very bad book, I know that now," Fero told me. Peter and Alicia had used it to make the cassette of English expressions for Alicia's grandfather so he could communicate with his Canadian émigré brother. They had been introduced to the text in their classes at Slovak Technical University, despite not being autodidacts in that setting. Clearly this was a historic document of English instruction in Slovakia. I wanted to own a copy, and Goran, who cherished the book, was understandably unwilling to part with his.

I remember I first "encountered" the book when I visited Goran's house in 1994 and introduced myself to his brother, who said memorably in return the only English words he knew: "It's a big orange." Apparently the phrase "It's a big orange" was *Angličtina pre Samoukov*'s lesson 1 on the "to be" verb, page 15.[1] When Goran and I reached the bookstore in Polus, he assured me the book would be in stock, adding that even though we would find a more recent edition than the one everyone had used before the end of the communist regime, "You will see it has not changed." "It's a big orange," he was certain, would still be there. Yet as we approached the shelf of English language textbooks, Goran's certainty began to wane. He was surprised to find the shelf stuffed with volumes similar in size and cover design and even title to his favorite *Angličtina pre Samoukov,* but by various authors. It took Goran a moment to locate Kollmannová's text, a version copyrighted in Slovak in 1997. Goran turned to lesson 1, page 15. The lesson on the "to be" verb was no longer "It's a big orange," but instead "Mr. Mitch is rich":

JOHNNY: You are rich, Mr. Mitch.

MR. MITCH: Oh no, I'm not. The garden isn't large, and the house is small and very old.

JOHNNY: But your car's new. It's nice and it's big.

MR. MITCH: This isn't my car. My old car's in the garage.[2]

Although lesson 1 was now devoted to this debate as to whether the resplendence of Mr. Mitch's new house and car was sufficient to qualify him as "rich," Mr. Mitch demurring at every conversational turn, I eventually located an orange further on in the text, there the subject of a cartoon shopping lesson. The cartoon depicts a tourist in London asking a vendor, "How much is an orange?" The fruit-stand vendor answers, "50p." The tourist, a savvy shopper, replies, "What? 50 pence? I can get an orange for 35p just round the corner."[3] To appreciate this change in the orange's position in the text—from its status as simple ontological subject in the early 1980s, to its postrevolutionary incarnation as object of fluctuating value—is to appreciate that much more is being taught in this lesson than English. The dialogue between vendor and consumer conveys the logic of commodification inherent to capitalism. One of the biggest complaints or delights about the end of socialism, depending upon one's vantage point, was that items no longer cost the same predictable amount. To help people navigate this phenomenon, newspapers in Bratislava by 2003 printed charts detailing the relative prices of bread, milk, and other common staples at supermarkets across the city. Thus people were taught to "shop around," because these commodities could be found at many places and prices. For this lesson in comparison shopping to be conveyed through an orange in the revised *Angličtina pre Samoukov* was particularly poignant, as under the communist regime, oranges were treasured commodities, the symbol of what one could not have except on rare occasions. Now, the book tells the reader, oranges can be gotten around the corner—for less.

Goran's favorite English textbook was not the only one in Slovakia to introduce postcommunist citizens to their roles in capitalism. The rudiments of capitalist logic were broadly put forth in lessons in English textbooks both foreign and domestic. Gone were the communist-era English language textbooks, typified by dialogues celebrating the achievements of striking workers abroad;[4] the new textbooks showcased the possibilities of the global spread of capitalism and were replete with reminders of the link between English and employment. English lessons were thus lessons in English's value to economic development and personal security. The sheer proliferation of textbooks carrying these lessons, however, conveyed the more unsettling message that anything could be commodified, even a language. Just like bread and milk, English could be peddled by a variety of vendors, in a variety of forms, at a variety of prices.[5] In this infinite variety, however, there was a catch, an aspect of capitalism—and English—that produced the hesitation I witnessed in Goran at the bookstore. Contrary to what Goran had imagined, in fact, Kollmannová's 1997 *Angličtina pre Samoukov* was cover to cover an almost entirely different book than the edition he had learned English from in the 1980s (perhaps the biggest distinction being the 1997 volume's sponsorship: an actual advertisement for one of Slovakia's many agencies offering students work-abroad opportunities in the United States appeared on the final page). Not only had the original changed, but many other *Angličtina pre Samoukov*'s had emerged—knockoffs designed to look just like the "one" that had been, yet at the same time paradoxically "new" and improved, as everything had to be in order to sell. If a cherished book could be commodified, then what, or more to the point who, couldn't be?

This question seemed to underlie, and temper, Slovakia's otherwise fervent embrace of both capitalism and English in the years leading up to 2004's European Union accession. Although textbooks foreign and domestic introduced both English and capitalism as imperatives, the domestic ones did so with a bit more hesitation and hedging—like Mr. Mitch they demurred, like Goran they paused, registering their ambivalence about capitalism and the changes it wrought. Many Slovaks were beginning to face capitalism's logic of built-in obsolescence, and they were facing it in English. The dictates of the fast-moving economy meant that to keep up, they had to multitask, often learning English after their long days at work or before their long days had begun.[6] English became the idiom of the postcommunist experience of job insecurity. In the fall of 2003, for example, an omnipresent life insurance ad in bus stops and on billboards featured the English word *Family* prominently, with accompanying Slovak text explaining what life insurance is. The text framed a photo of a young girl in swimming attire with three life preservers around her body. Life insurance, a new commodity in the postcommunist era, bespoke the privatization of social security.[7] The branding of this new kind of security was achieved through English, as was the branding of a not so easily commodified element of Western capitalism: the new, visible homeless population, dubbed in young Slovaks' growing lexicon of Slovak-English slang as "homelessak."

When I spoke with people in postcommunist Slovakia, however, I found that the greatest anxiety was actually not that of winding up on the street, but rather the more modest fear of falling behind, of failing to capitalize on opportunities. This fear, the inevitable companion of the idioms of "improvement" and "bettering oneself" continually attached to English, reveals a paradox of global English as the language of capitalism: On the one hand, while English must ever portray itself as standardized in order for people to buy into it as the medium for commodification and trade, it really only attracts people by commodifying distinction; learn me, it beckons, and you will know things that the others don't. Don't learn me, and you will be the one not to know.

This paradox, indicative of the asymmetries of information inherent to capitalism in practice, is initially unpacked here through stories in which the narrative of English as "betterment" is constantly dogged by the specter of job insecurity. First we meet two employees of Goran's company: Viola, a sales associate whose attempt to "keep up" with other Slovaks' standard of living meant switching jobs and switching Englishes; and her boyfriend, Ruslan, a service technician who squeezed English lessons into his unforgiving schedule to stay afloat at the job he had held for nearly a decade. Next we will meet Iveta, a freelance English teacher, and her husband, whose stories demonstrate that although the global economy presented the inflexible imperative to learn English, people themselves had to become very flexible in order to fulfill this imperative. A comparison of domestic and foreign materials and spaces for learning English follows, showing how anxieties over learning English translated into ambivalent lessons in domestic textbooks. Lastly I return to Jan, the corporate lawyer, and introduce Pavol, a representative of Slovakia's police department to the EU, both troubled by the instability of English, wondering how they could retain some form of ownership over the English they had taken pains to acquire as they looked forward to working less someday.

KEEPING UP

On November 17, 2003, the fourteenth anniversary of the official end of communism in Slovakia, one could hear a pin drop in the main square of Bratislava. It was a bank holiday, but otherwise the day passed with little official acknowledgment. The National Bank of Slovakia, then the tallest building in the city, had left all its lights on at night in commemoration—an unpopular move that did little to promote cheer. As Maria explained, cash-strapped Bratislava residents regarded their national bank's gesture with some suspicion, seeing their own crowns wasted on the display. Enunciating growing discontent with the process of economic reform, Robert Fico, the leader of the Social Democracy party Smer (and by 2006, prime minister), publicly remarked that people had been better off during communism.[8] When I mentioned his comment to Viola, she remarked, "Oh please," adding, "I can hardly imagine that from now until Christmas I will stand in line to buy oranges. When I was young my family—my mother, my father, my brother, and me—had to stand in line behind each other for two hours, not talking to each other, to buy four kilos of oranges because each person was only allowed one kilo. We had the money, but there was nothing to buy."

Viola did not like the practice during the communist regime of parceling out oranges, English, or anything else in deference to arbitrary rules bearing no relationship to demand. When the revolution occurred midway through Viola's high school career, she and other students in her *gymnázium* in the moderate-sized city of Nitra "demanded" more English. Emphasizing that the urge to study English was not imposed from without, Viola added, "We started to learn English because it was our decision." She recalled her own and her fellow students' embrace of what they saw as real-world English instruction—lessons that revolved around translating British and American pop songs and watching CNN broadcasts.

Viola, however, quickly went after graduation from feeling ahead of the growing countrywide fascination with English to feeling as though she was falling behind. The knowledge of English she had gained in *gymnázium* proved only somewhat useful in her later courses at Slovakia's most prestigious university, Komenius, where she went to study biology. The approach at Komenius toward English instruction seemed to her to encourage survival of the already prepared; despite the fact that all the biology books and materials provided to students were in English, she was offered only one semester of optional English, with forty students in the class. She refined her reading knowledge of specialized scientific vocabulary in English largely through her own efforts, yet she found herself lagging behind others in her cohort who could understand the influx of foreign students and foreign movies. Feeling out of the loop, she started taking English courses at a private academy twice a week. However, Viola was a student with no money, earning what little she could by working in a factory on weekends, and English lessons proved to be a luxury she could not long afford.

After receiving her degree in 1995, Viola worked for the Institute of Biology at the Slovak Academy of Sciences for one year, during which she used her reading knowledge of English nearly daily. Officially her job was researching rodents as disease vectors, but her opportunities to conduct primary research were frustratingly spare.[9] Laboratory science in Slovakia was highly reliant on foreign investment; without assistance from foreign universities, researchers in Slovakia faced continual shortages of chemicals and other necessary laboratory materials. Little had been done in the 1990s to address years of stagnation of scientific research in the country. Day after day there would be nothing new for Viola to do at the lab but read journal articles in English and take notes. After one year she determined that she couldn't survive in Bratislava on the salary she made, much less save money: "I told myself I'm young, I'm single, I have no children, so I have some time to do some career to improve myself."

Viola's notion that she could "improve herself" was, she made clear, one that could only have emerged with the end of the communist regime. Improving one's circumstances during the communist regime—legally—

was rarely an option, and the idea of striving to excel was also strongly discouraged. Viola summed up what she had learned in school: "Usually people taught in school to small children that capitalism is very bad, USA is very bad, socialism is very good, and everyone is in the same level, nobody will have more money than another. Even if you were more clever or more successful in your job . . . you have to be the same than the other people. Socialists usually say no differences between people. And now situation changed. It was possible to show that you were cleverer, more successful in some things."

Young, female, single, and able to consider radically different careers (and surpass her peers in pay), Viola was part of a demographic that had emerged in Slovakia after 1989. Before then, there had been great incentive for women to marry early, generally to gain one's own apartment and shorter military service for one's spouse. Beginning in the 1990s, however, Slovakia experienced a sharp decline in both marriage and birth rates and an increase in the age of first-time mothers, as young women began to explore their options rather than settling down to raise a family in their early twenties.[10] Settling down, however, had also itself become a challenging endeavor. The newfound social freedoms were accompanied by skyrocketing real estate prices that made it difficult for young people to afford housing, particularly in Bratislava.[11] Whereas before 1989 young people could receive a state flat, no such guarantees existed after rampant privatization.

Viola acknowledged that after the Velvet Revolution she was under great pressure to earn more money to have the basics—food, clothes, health care, and shelter—that she would not have had to worry about under the communist regime. But she was now after not simply the basics, but a sense of betterment. She speculated that if she had finished college before 1989 and embarked on her career back then, "Maybe I would be satisfied to be a biologist, to have the salary according to some rules because the others would be in the same situation." Her comment about how she might have performed in relationship to others suggests that the economic transformation provoked her to change careers not only to fulfill needs but to keep up with or surpass a newly stratifying set of peers.

Viola resigned herself to the reality that she would never improve on her financial situation if she remained a scientist. Looking to put her bi-

> Mr. Prokop cannot speak English. He can say hallo, goodbye, good night,
> but that is all. Now he has a new job in the export section of his firm and
> he must be able to speak and write English. Mr. Prokop can see that it is
> necessary to go to the language school. He must learn English there in
> Evening classes.
>
> —Eva Zábojová, Jaroslav Peprník, and Stella Nangonová, *Angličtina I.*
>   *Pre Samoukov a Kurzy*

ology training to work in the private sector, she applied for a position in
sales with Goran's firm. One of the requirements of the job was that she
"speak English fluently" so she could communicate with the firm's international partners. She promised Goran that although she didn't speak
very well, she would "improve." Once on the job, she had little time to
make the promised improvements before she was embroiled in situations
that taxed her narrow reading knowledge of English. She had learned English in university through scientific subjects; she had learned it through
movies, television, advertisements, and CNN. Yet now she was faced with
"business English. It was another type of words." Her unfamiliarity with
this "type of words" left her unable to communicate with American and
British clients: "I was not able to say one word! . . . I was shaking every time
the phone started to ring." She began studying at night from a textbook
but made little progress, usually too exhausted to concentrate at the end of
the day. Finally, in 2001, she engaged the services of a private tutor at her
own expense and learned to speak the words of global economic parlance.
By 2003 she had held the position in the firm for seven years. "I was still
shaking," she said, "for five years."

STAYING AFLOAT

While Viola was hired with the expectation that she would learn English
fluently, other members of the company who were not in sales, or who had
been working there for years, had not been hired with such an expectation.
Increasingly, however, not knowing English was no longer an option even
for them. As Goran explained, by 2003 almost 80 percent of his company's
business was with American clients; six or seven years earlier, his business

had been predominantly with German clients. Given the shift in clientele, 60 or 70 percent of Goran's staff had to know English at some level. "Somebody has to speak fluently, somebody has to at least speak," Goran explained. His business model, insofar as English was concerned, embodied hierarchy and specialization.

Ruslan, a friend of Goran's from adolescence and Viola's boyfriend since shortly after she had joined the firm, was one of those not obliged to know any English when he was first hired as a service technician. And in fact, he did not know any. Even though his business card announced his position in both English and Slovak, few of the clients he saw probably read the English: his duties involved constant travel, but virtually all of it was domestic. When I saw Ruslan in August 2003, however, he had nine months to learn enough English to take part in a training session for new machinery, scheduled to take place at the headquarters of one of Goran's American suppliers. Since Goran's company did not hire English teachers to teach employees, Ruslan would have to acquire the language on his own.

I had first met Ruslan in 1994 at Goran's house. At that time we were barely able to communicate: he knew no English, and I had picked up only rudimentary Slovak. When we met again in 2003, he approached me to ask if he could hire me to teach him English. He had no time to take a course, he explained, due to his frequent trips out of town. I said I'd be happy to teach him for nothing because I would learn from the experience as well, but he would not allow it. He suggested we meet during his rare free time, over dinner (on him), after he returned from service calls. The restaurant where we met became our study hall; we worked through grammar and conversation as we worked through dinner. It was an extremely fluid arrangement, subject to the vagaries of both my schedule and his. Often we would plan to meet, only to find out on the day of our lesson that Ruslan was being sent to Eastern Slovakia to repair a piece of machinery.

Goran, meanwhile, had a stake in Ruslan's efforts, and he asked me how Ruslan was doing—principally if he would be on track to attend the training in America in April. I produced the full disclosure: although Ruslan had progressed, he would need more than me to be prepared for the trip. Goran smiled and said that Ruslan was "soft, like jelly," suggesting that Ruslan lacked the resolve to follow through. It had become Goran's philosophy that everyone in Slovakia needed to learn English if the country was to compete in the global marketplace. In his view, the only things stalling this process were insufficient motivation and the mistaken belief that German was more useful. I suggested that Ruslan's unpredictable schedule, entailing service calls all around Slovakia, meant he couldn't know if he had free time for a lesson until one day before. Without time, he would never learn enough English to take part in the training.

The following week, I met with Ruslan in our usual restaurant. As we sat down, Ruslan asked me, with rare fluency but a somewhat puzzled expression, "What did you say to [Goran]?" Apparently, in the intervening week, Ruslan had been enrolled in an intensive English course, four nights a week for two hours each session, for a total of forty-eight hours of class time (at his expense—though, we calculated, at a cheaper rate than buying me dinner). Goran had arranged for other people to cover Ruslan's service calls outside the Bratislava area so he could attend the course. Ruslan, over the next month, threw himself into the lessons. He started listening to the BBC, according to his Slovak English teacher's recommendation, while he drove to service calls. At home he drove Viola crazy by insisting that they speak English when they were together. Periodically he called me up to read his homework over the phone, with achingly correct intonation. In the end, the training was moved to Europe, where it would probably take place in German. Nevertheless, Ruslan's English lessons continued, according to Goran's vision of a future in which everyone would study English: "No other way," Goran explained of the imperative to study English. "I don't know who can change it. It will be the international language or second language for everybody." Goran, the most traveled member of the company, had come to view Slovakia as being in the grip of international forces, with no choice other than to keep up.

KITCHEN STORY

Iveta, like Viola, found herself swept up after graduation from college by the growing corporate hunger for English instruction, though as a teacher, not as a student. Just a few years younger than Viola, Iveta had begun her study of English during the communist regime, at the age of eleven, somewhat serendipitously. She could only start taking English classes because some other students had dropped out of an accelerated curriculum offered only to a select number, and she was approached to fill one of the empty spaces. She explained: "It was not just English, but it was the opportunity to be better in some way, because the class was considered to be elite in the school. It wasn't just English, it was a bonus, something extra I could get." In spite of the formal ideology of equality, such special classes existed; Iveta saw a rare chance to get something "extra" and grabbed it.

Later in life Iveta, with similar rapidity, adapted to the new economic terrain. She studied English and biology in a teacher-training course at the same university as Fero (which is how they met). After graduation from university, Iveta spent a year in England teaching biology in a private secondary school; however, on her return to Slovakia, she sought work teaching English exclusively in a private language academy serving companies. She expected to be hired as a full-time employee, but she instead encountered the new rules of flexible labor arrangements and decreasing job security. She was asked to get her own license to work at the language school so she would be self-employed and only paid for the classes she taught. "I was kind of forced into that," she said of the arrangement. Yet she soon found ways to turn the new rules of English language instruction in Slovakia to her advantage, her most profitable work freelancing for companies and taking on private students. She found there was no shortage of companies needing her services; many, regardless of what country they were based in, had adopted English as their official language: "Mostly they were companies owned by foreign investors, so people needed English to communicate with their counterparts in Germany, for example." Noting the new imperative to learn English for many of her students, she observed: "With some of them it was a precondition to speak English to stay in their positions. . . . For some of them it was really difficult, so they would give up and would have to start again." It was a "never-ending story," she added ruefully, highlighting the situation of her students—and, indeed, many in Slovakia. The irony here is that Iveta, a master of English with no job security, repeatedly faced a classroom full of students hoping to secure their own jobs by learning the English she proffered.

Iveta changed her job again to a position that entailed teaching business English to students in the Economics Department of the university where she had gotten her degree. Although this job was less lucrative than

> Many supermarkets in the U.S.A. are outside big cities because the rent there is cheaper. Shoppers come in their cars, leave the car in a large parking lot at the supermarket, and then take their shopping in a cart or in a large brown paper bag to the car. The prices of the same dresses, shirts, etc. are often higher in downtown stores than in the suburbs. Sometimes you find the sign "Sale" on the shop windows. This means that the goods will be cheaper for a week or two.
>
> —Eva Zábojová, Jaroslav Peprník, and Stella Nangonová, *Angličtina I.*
>   *Pre Samoukov a Kurzy*

teaching for corporations, Iveta felt she needed to develop her own English skills, which she worried might otherwise atrophy. Like Viola, she perceived that survival in the new economic terrain was a matter of self-improvement, so her pursuit of English needed to be a "never-ending story" as well. The very novelty of the economic transformations the country was undergoing, which had led so many of her students back to English, made her new job—teaching English through the subject of economics—just the challenge she had been looking for: "I was fed up with just teaching English. I wanted to discuss different things with people. . . . Business is not such a specific subject, it's very broad, it's changing. There are many new things, many new ideas."[12] Given the speed with which the business world moved, her main teaching materials came from the Internet, particularly articles from the online version of the *Financial Times.* (Downloads of current articles were also much more affordable for students and schools than textbooks would have been.) She found her new position intellectually satisfying, yet she also found herself stuck in a new way. In order to advance in her position, she would need to do research she had no time to do, and she would never make much money. When we spoke, she was considering leaving her job to found a bilingual *gymnázium*—possibly in collaboration with Fero and Zlatica. Weighing the chances of such a venture succeeding, Iveta pondered the market for English language teaching and what niche her school could fill: "The market is full of language schools that teach only language, but there is no opportunity for students to learn something in English." She concluded that they would need to offer some form of specialized English in order to distinguish themselves.

As I sat talking with Iveta in her flat on the outskirts of Banská Bystrica, in a block-style apartment building with a view of grazing sheep and the mountains beyond, I had to note that the most telling indication of how English had come to permeate the lives and job prospects of so many could be found in her kitchen. English expressions had been scribbled in black marker on almost every inch of her kitchen cupboards. Some were accompanied by Slovak translations, and some were not. The majority of these expressions were economic, and many—like *bond, stock market,* and *redundancy payment*—had no translation. Apparently the scribbler was not Iveta, but her husband, Martin, a manager at a major supermarket chain who had listened to the BBC on the radio every morning (when it was still available) and paused during breakfast preparations to jot down some of the phrases used on the program so he could learn them. "He's hoping to get a better job someday," she explained.

Iveta's cabinets embodied the belief in English as a pathway to economic mobility—a belief she, her students, and her corporate partners all held in common. They spoke to the change in the kind of English people learned, an English that introduced people to economic liberalism. But

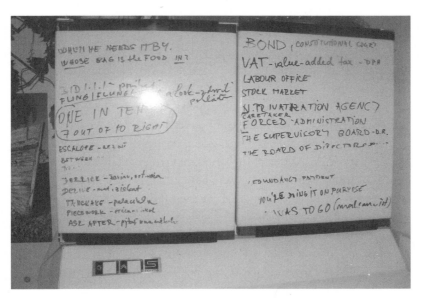

FIG. 2. Iveta's cabinets. Photograph by Zuzana Ličková.

they also spoke to how English had permeated not just the business office but, through it, day-to-day life, such that the mundane activities of making coffee and doing dishes were now intermingled with lessons in English and capitalism. I tried to imagine the juggling Iveta's husband went through in the morning: how did he maneuver around the kitchen with both milk and marker in hand?

A MODEST PLACE

If there was any industry where jobs seemed assured in postcommunist Slovakia, it was the auto industry. By 2003, Volkswagen, Citroën, and Kia had all either built or were planning to build a plant in Slovakia to take advantage of the country's relatively inexpensive but educated labor force. Much of this force would be educated at Slovak Technical University (STU), the institution hosting my research. The language faculty of STU were well aware that their students would need more preparation for some of these jobs than a basic text like *Angličtina pre Samoukov* would provide. In 1999 they enrolled in a workshop with the British Council to revise their materials and emerged with *English for Students of Mechanical Engineering,* which introduced vocabulary and expressions pertinent to mechanical engineers alongside instruction in the fundamentals of Western capitalism. Lessons from this text were just as likely to revolve around advertisements and cover letters as around descriptions of engines. Readings introduced students to the dynamics of unemployment (which in Slovakia, in 2002, had crept up to nearly 20 percent) and explained that when unemployment is high, there might be many applicants for one position.[13] "Jobs for Life? Not Anymore," one passage announced.

This last message was underscored in the lesson introducing the Western-style CV. As one of the language faculty at STU told me, under the communist regime the CV was a biographical essay in which students were required to reveal their parents' names. If their parents were working-class, that was great; however, if they were white-collar, the applicant's prospects were lower. The main rhetorical task the writer of the old CV faced, therefore, was to foreground someone in the family, however distantly related, who was a factory worker. The old CV also routinely featured other personal information, such as birthday, marital status, and nationality.[14]

The department head was concerned that he, like many of the other faculty who had come of age under the communist regime, was ill equipped to introduce students to the new conventions of employment in the Western world. In fact, the Western-style CV sample in *English for Students of Mechanical Engineering* (last updated in 2001) still displayed date of birth, sex, marital status, and nationality. The language faculty knew that their sample should be revised, but they were in a quandary: STU had little money to fund a further edition of the text, and the materials needed to print new textbooks were almost prohibitively expensive. Their CV was more current, however, in foregrounding the importance of certification in English. Under the "skills" heading the CV boasts: "Proficiency in English (British Council, First Cambridge Certificate Course—1999)."[15] The British Council and Cambridge's First Certificate were prominently displayed elsewhere in *English for Students* as well: the book's sample letter is addressed to the British Council, asking for information about programs leading to the First Certificate in English. Knowledge of English in and of itself is no longer enough, the STU textbook suggests. English fluency must now be certified and credentialized—preferably by an international agency—before it can gain its full value.

One might wonder why Slovak Technical University would list the British Council Certificate on its sample CV, particularly when the university had its own private language academy and thus might be seen as lending press to a competitor in the profitable private English instruction market. The answer is that the British Council really faced no credible internal threat to its hegemonic position in this market.[16] The physical spaces that house STU and the British Council, respectively, indicate the advantages the British Council enjoyed as the well-funded cultural arm of an affluent country. Even though Slovak Technical University was preparing students for Slovakia's most promising economic sector, it had not, as a state institution, prospered with the advent of capitalism. Although the English language faculty at the mechanical engineering college had hoped that their own job security would be one of the outcomes of the growth in Slovakia's auto industry, by 2003 they had witnessed only declines in state funding. Books and other instructional materials remained scarce. What new money did come to the college came from abroad: its Internet service was provided through a partnership with Austria; the sculpture in

---

Ask questions to match these answers:

1. I want to speak English fluently.

2. Because I need it for my job.

—Anna Kucharíková, Kevin Slavin, and Jozef Galata, *English for Students of Mechanical Engineering*

---

the lobby was a giant Volkswagen with its guts exposed, rolled up against a Soviet-era tableau of industrial landscapes. Foreign investment proved a mixed blessing for the universities, however: tax breaks given to corporations coming into Slovakia were in part responsible for the decline in funding of state-run universities. To address this decline in tax revenue, the minister of education had proposed instituting tuition, a reform that caused parents and students great anxiety.

The British Council was both a short walk and a world away. If one exited the STU lobby doors, turned left, and headed down to the historic district, one would find the British Council nestled among upscale Western boutiques, right across from the British Consulate, where in the fall of 2003, just months shy of EU accession, Slovaks lined up to apply for visas to travel to Britain. The council's building, in Bratislava's historic "Old Town," had been updated to provide modern conveniences yet preserved a Gothic arch from the original construction behind glass in the stairwell. The second floor featured an elegant meeting hall with carved wooden ceilings and walls. Books on pedagogy, magazines, newspapers, and DVDs and videos in English were abundantly available. Among these materials was a popular series of English language teaching texts by Longman (also adopted by some Slovak schools in 2003) entitled *Opportunities.* This title suggests the connection between learning English and capitalizing on the opportunities, large and small, of the capitalist world, as do the textbook's lessons instructing students how to bargain in English and when not to just buy at the advertised price. *Opportunities* represented Slovak Technical University's competition—a text that was full of color images from Hollywood movies: permissions and photos and print stock that STU could never dream of affording. The authors of *English for Students of Mechanical Engineering* acknowledge in their preface that course materials were now available that were "pleasing to the eye": in an addendum to this acknowledgment reminiscent of Mr. Mitch's demurrals, they express the hope that their text would take its "modest place" among such materials. This modesty seems a tacit recognition that a text like *Opportunities* is not only more pleasing but also a step ahead in the process of commodification. Longman was selling not a niche type of English, but an abstraction: opportunity. The word "English" doesn't even appear on the cover.

The authors of the STU text also acknowledge that their students had changed since 1989, now entering university with "the pragmatic desire to make their way forward in a world where English, for better or worse, has become an indispensable tool." This "for better or worse," while clearly ambivalent, is also ambiguous. Better why? Worse for whom? For clarity we must turn elsewhere, specifically to Jan and Pavol, whose thoughts on global English illuminated this ambivalence, demonstrating that in a world of goods undergoing a process of commodification, the distinction of being "in the know" through English had become the most valuable property one could "own."

THE KINGS AND THE BLIND

At first glance, Jan and Pavol would seem quite different. While Jan was building a palatial house and driving custom cars, Pavol, also approximately forty years old, lived with a roommate in a policeman's dormitory and drove a decades-old Škoda whose only adornment was a crucifix swinging from the rearview mirror. Pavol was seemingly impervious to the consumerism spreading through Bratislava, his main vices in terms of consumption cigarettes and photography equipment. Nonetheless, Pavol and Jan (who never met) were of the same mind: communism had been one of the most destructive forces of the twentieth century, and capitalism was a vast improvement.[17]

Pavol memorably remarked of teaching English in Slovakia, "Best business I've done since stamp collecting." During communism, however, English had been of little value to him beyond being an interesting hobby. He stopped studying it after high school, when it became clear to him he might never be able to leave the country. Born in 1963 in a small industrial town in southern Slovakia, Pavol recalled of beginning English lessons in school: "I remember the teacher asked, 'Who wants to study English?' We raised our hands up. And he counted one, two, three, thirteen, that's all, you know? The other students had to study German. They *all* wanted to study English. No choice. . . . It depended on how quick you were, how quickly you managed to raise your hand. It was a kind of sport." On the Communist Party's blacklist because of his and his family's overt Christianity, Pavol didn't try to attend university until the regime collapsed. He then went and graduated as an English teacher. When I met him in 2003, he was teaching night courses through Slovak Technical University's private language school, but with an intriguing day job: police officer. Four years previously, Pavol had taken a position at the Traffic Police Department of Foreign Relations, where his duties quickly exceeded the job of teaching a largely recalcitrant force. He began not only commenting on traffic law proposals for the European Union and the United Nations but also representing the Slovak Republic in working groups at international conferences. In this position he traveled about six times a year: twice to Geneva for the UN agenda, twice to Brussels for the EU agenda, and twice with the Organization for Economic Co-operation and Development (OECD).[18] I asked him if he had any qualifications for police work and traffic control besides knowing English. He replied: "I think this was the main precondition, because, you know, in Slovakia you say, 'The one-eyed is the king among the blind' [Jednooký je medzi slepými kráľom]. So I'm the only person who can speak English in the traffic police department. Or at least I can speak at that level that I can use specialized English, and I can speak at meetings and translate."

This specialized English proved to be a precious commodity for Pavol. It made him metaphorically "king" in an area in which he was a relative newcomer, putting him in a position to affect national and to some extent international traffic policy. It is also interesting to note, however, how the new status of English, which had made Pavol "king," had simultaneously rendered the other people in his department "blind." Describing how English kept him in the know and others out of it, he spoke of how information from the EU filtered to him before anyone else: "EU announced the road safety as a priority, but no one knows here, but you and me."

Pavol, however, was not content resting on these laurels of distinction. From his position in the international realm, he was able to witness varieties of global English emerging, and they worried him. Chiefly he was concerned that English was in danger of becoming a commodity in the cheapest sense of the term—quality and tradition in English usage would go out the window as new varieties competed for airtime. As he put it, "Maybe at this international level, there is a British, American, Australian English, and an international language." He parsed the international variant further to include European English, which he blamed for the deterioration of his skills in British English. But he also worried that "vulgarization" of English by foreigners would lead to fragmentation rather than a lingua franca. He explained: "There is a danger, you know. In old Latin, in the beginning it was only for very educated people. They could use it in the proper way. But Latin in the course of time vulgarized, because there were more people who used Latin and transferred their language into the Latin. And suddenly I think—I'm not sure whether I'm right—they couldn't understand each other. This is why Latin died. . . . What is the danger [with English] is that we will stop understanding the native speakers." As linguist Robert Phillipson observes, parallels drawn between English and Latin fall short on several accounts, but particularly because they do not recognize that English is imbued with capitalism. Embedded in Pavol's views about international English and its uses, however, was an implicit (and decidedly antisocialist) argument about property: that languages for their own good should not be everyone's property. Pavol's sense of linguistic property relations seemed to be analogous to the tragedy of the commons, where a resource that becomes available to an unlimited number of users (in this case the English language; in the classic case a grazing field) is eventually ruined through overuse as each person tries to maximize his own potential gain. Just as the example of the destroyed grazing field has often been invoked to argue for private property, Pavol's comparison of English to Latin was meant to argue for the limited spread of English so that its meaning would be preserved and so that those who studied it centuries from now would still understand native speakers. Without some kings, his argument suggested, we would all be blind.

Where Pavol saw net loss in a de-Anglicized English, Jan saw net gain. Jan, as a corporate lawyer specializing in international mergers, also distinguished an international variant of English from the English spoken in Britain or America, and he too harbored a conception of English as a lingua franca that would function in international communication. His beliefs about English were grounded, however, in his calculations of what would help him compete with others. He understood that knowledge of a language could make or break fortunes because it had played a pivotal role in creating his own. Jan told me that when the business codes of the country were rewritten in 1991 to suit Western Europe, the effect was a nullification of the seniority of lawyers within Slovakia. Suddenly all lawyers were on the same level, all blind, starting from the same place with essentially the same amount of relevant experience (i.e., little). According to Jan, those who were young, who were not afraid of computers, and who knew English and German could move up very quickly. Jan rose to become a member of the emerging landlord class, with investments to protect. His concern for the fair ability to compete, not just communicate, in the international arena was reflected in his thoughts about English. Here is where he and Pavol differed: Jan worried about the vulgarization of English from within England, not from without.

Unlike Pavol, who placed the burden of comprehensibility on newcomers to English, Jan placed it squarely on the British. The British, he felt, should not use any local jargon or excessively idiomatic expressions and should strive as much as possible for what he considered a "neutral" accent; ironically, given his desire to wrest English from British control, he nevertheless identified this accent as BBC English (no doubt more identifiable to Jan as "neutral" because he had spent extensive time in England; Pavol, in contrast, preferred the American accent). Jan's exhibit A of the problematic British English speaker was Liza, a friend of Peter and Alicia's whom I had taught with in 1992 and 1994. Liza hailed from Newcastle, England, but had spent most of her adult life in theater administration in London's West End before moving to Slovakia in 1991. Because her parents were Czech Jewish emigrants who had escaped persecution and grown up in Sweden, she viewed her return to Czechoslovakia in 1990 (initially via Education for Democracy) a return home. It was Liza's view that the BBC World Service was archaic and completely unrepresentative of how actual British people spoke. And, indeed, her speech was peppered with the kind of phrases that would not likely appear on the BBC.

Liza's English annoyed Jan to no end. As he saw it, by speaking the vernacular of Newcastle, Liza was engaging in the linguistic equivalent of squatting on public property. Jan often implored her, "Speak English," and she just as often responded, "I am speaking English." Recounting an apparently frequent argument they had, Jan made out his case for a transparent English in terms of ownership and property rights: "I was telling her that the British do not own the language. . . . I was asking her to speak some neutral, clean BBC English. . . . She told me there is no such a thing as BBC English at all, that the language as such is not codified, that the English language is a live and still developing thing, and the proper way to speak the language is the way it is spoken in England. . . . I told her that English is not the property of England. English is an international language." Remembering well Jan's fascination with cockney English in 1994, I was initially surprised at the strength of his rejection of vernacular English. But then again, what he had liked about cockney was that it was a kind of a code, and he knew it. Now he was beginning to feel codes working against him. For Jan, English was a powerful and even essential resource, a form of information that must belong to everyone, not just native speakers. In his view it was the responsibility of native speakers to "buy into" an English that the world could understand. His insistence on clarity was understandable coming from someone who lived or died by the subtle word, the nuance that creates the loophole. In the specialized English he had mastered—the law—the creation of information "noise," or lack of transparency, was key. He felt that British nationals frequently created such noise with their vernaculars to maintain an unfair advantage. He complained of one international conference he had attended: "The English, maybe even on purpose, they spoke in a way that was very difficult for the others. And this isn't right."

Jan's "right" indicates that besides the discourse of ownership, there is another common terminology between Jan and Pavol: they both invoked propriety. Indeed, both used the word "proper." When Pavol drew his analogy between English and Latin, he said, "They could use it in the proper way." Jan recounted Liza's assertion that "the proper way to speak the language is the way it is spoken in England" and his response that "English is not the property of England." It is no accident that *property* and *propriety* have the same Latin root: *proprietas.* If propriety is about convention, it is just as much about distinguishing oneself from the "improper."

Although Jan and Pavol felt the threats to propriety coming from different directions, they both worried about losing the distinction of "knowing" something others didn't. In the new capitalist logic, in which information had become the most precious commodity, this form of distinction had become the most valuable property of all.

Here Jan's and Pavol's age—both a full decade older than Viola and Iveta—is significant. Both were finished chasing betterment and English. Pavol, when I met him, had just declined a slightly higher-paying job offer from the Financial Police Department. He explained: "I'd have to change everything, my vocabulary. . . . It's not easy for me to learn. I'm a forty-year-old man." Jan hoped to retire imminently, seeing no point in a lifetime career. "Working for a living is the stupidest way to make money," he told me once. Jan understood capitalist logic perfectly.

The sense of "bettering oneself" through English carries an obvious moral ring—and has carried it historically and widely. There was, however, in the postcommunist environment, still another morality—one that stood for social security—that challenged the capitalist moral logic; the resulting competition produced the ambivalence I witnessed in so many Slovak-produced English textbooks. A reading from a 2000 volume entitled *Angličtina I. pre Samoukov a Kurzy* (which looks, of course, a lot like Kollmannová's text), for example, skeptically presents the lifelong chase after security presented by integration with the capitalist West. The authors observe: "In the U.S.A. the retirement age was raised in 1978 to seventy for men and to sixty-five for women; for civil servants there is no age limit at all. Of course they can retire earlier if they like, but with a smaller retirement program. The Americans say that in this way the wide experience of old workers can be used longer. In the Slovak Republic men retire at the age of sixty. . . . We believe that with an earlier retirement age young people get an earlier opportunity to be in responsible jobs. . . . Besides, after forty years of work a person deserves a rest, doesn't he?"[19] By the year 2001 in Slovakia, the maximum retirement benefit of 8,282 Slovak crowns (for miners who had worked a minimum of fifteen years) amounted to under 300 dollars a month—or a few hundred crowns more than the cost of a course in English at the British Council in 2003.[20] Not much of a rest could be had on that, and so we might imagine that many

Slovaks read with some irony the closing dialogue of Kollmannová's 1997 *Angličtina pre Samoukov,* in which a young woman tells an old man sitting on a park bench, "We live and learn." The old man responds, book in hand, "No one is too old to . . . to . . . to learn!"[21]

4   Real Life in English

O f all the artifacts I collected in 2003, one is particularly evocative of the paradoxes and ambiguities of English in postcommunist Slovakia: my certificate of completion of the twenty-five-hour course "Principals and Practice of National Testing IV in the Framework of the Project 'Reform of the Slovak Maturita.'" The certificate bears my name and title—"Catherine PRENDERGAST, PhD"—as well as the signatures of the foreign consultant and native speaker of English hired to teach the course, and the director of the office of the Ministry of Education concerned with the reform.[1] No fewer than five logos stake their territory in various spots on the certificate: the logo of the Ministry; the seal of the Slovak Republic; the logos of the British Council and George Soros's Open Society Foundation (the two organizations financing the course and much of the reform); and last, the logo for the "maturita," or national high school graduation exam—that logo a check in a circle next to the word "Maturita." The certificate, in short, is the picture of official sanction, folded in thick blue laminated paper stock, draped ceremonially with a thin rope in the colors of the Slovak state.

I begin with this certificate because its overkill of logos is emblematic: the story I'm about to relate—that of the reform of Slovakia's maturita in English—is one in which foreign and domestic agencies, individual desires, politics, economics, and English all collide within a markedly small space. Before pulling apart the various elements of this collision to examine them one by one, however, I'd like to note that the pomp of the certificate stands out in stark contrast to the circumstance of how I came by it: Early on in my research in Slovakia, I discovered through British Council promotional materials that a team had been assembled, with British Council support, to reform the maturita in English. I emailed the particular institute of the Ministry involved in the effort and asked if I could observe the team's upcoming meeting, the purpose of which was allegedly to redesign the speaking portion of the exam under the guidance of a consultant (provided by the British Council). In my email I described my research, my university affiliation, and my presence in Slovakia under the auspices of the Council for the International Exchange of Scholars. The Ministry immediately responded that it would be helpful to have me around. Even though I had been forthright about my intention to publish a report based on my observations, I was not asked to keep any material related to the meeting "off the record." I was surprised that after only a one-sentence description of my research, I was invited to participate in the meeting to reform Slovakia's national graduation exam in English. This spoke to a certain eagerness to harness the resource of educational expertise from the West. But, as I found out, the ease with which I joined the meeting was also an indication that the real work of exam construction was happening elsewhere.

Before the meeting took place, Fero introduced me to a member of the maturita team who would further augur what I would be seeing— and not seeing—of the reform. A university trainer of secondary school teachers, Martina had become involved in the reform due to her expertise in testing and evaluation. Very welcoming of my interest in the maturita, she not only granted me an interview but also provided me a lift to the considerably distant meeting site: a sixteenth-century Renaissance manor (surrounded, appropriately enough for the occasion, by English-style gardens) that had been converted into a conference center and hotel. During our initial interview in her living room the day before we left for the meeting, Martina gave me the rough outlines of the reform to date. The goal was to take the traditional, as she put it, "subjective" maturita in English and make it an objective, internationally recognized exam. Not only was the new exam to be objective; it was also to assess the English knowledge of the postrevolution student, who, unlike the student of the communist regime, would no doubt have to use the language in the capitalist global order. The maturita, like every other aspect of English in Slovakia, was fragmenting into varieties to prepare students for the specific niches of this order. No longer was the test to be given at only one level. Part of the reform entailed giving students the choice of taking a lower- or upper-level exam. Martina told me that the writing task for the lower-level maturita had already been devised at the team's last meeting. It involved a "real-life" stimulus quite unlike anything that would have appeared in former versions of the maturita: students would be presented with an advertisement for a job and would have to write an application letter with, as she put it, "the proper form." In short, the "real-life" exercise the team had constructed engaged students in the practice of the capitalist job search. The writing task for the upper level, Martina told me, had not yet been written, but it would be an essay-writing task similar to those appearing on maturita exams of the past. In the meeting I was to observe, the team would construct the tasks, scales, and assessments for the speaking portion of the test.

Such was the agenda as Martina related it to me; however, several moments during our conversation left me uncertain. For someone participating in the reform of the maturita, Martina seemed a little fuzzy on its history and present status. At one point I showed Martina a textbook on preparing for the "new maturita" that I had seen teachers in secondary schools embracing as the guidebook to the upcoming exams. Although Martina knew the first author of the book as one of the coordinators of the reform team, she'd never seen the book before. She was also unsure about the genesis of the reform; she thought it might have begun in 1996 at a meeting of an association of teachers of English in the city of Poprad, but "maybe," she qualified, "maybe" it began even before that, the impetus coming from the influence of foreign lecturers who perceived weaknesses in the traditional maturita: "I'm not sure."

Martina's "I'm not sure" enunciates my own uncertainty as I embark on this chapter. The story of the maturita reform is a confusing one because it is a story about confusion. The meeting of the reform team I observed was fraught, its very purpose debated, grappled with, hashed out, and eventually decried. The thirteen people assembled weren't sure why they were there. Had they come together to write the exam, to serve as an advisory board to others (never fully identified) making the decisions, to receive training in an exam already constructed, or—a concern often expressed—to be players in a drama of no consequence whatsoever? The disquiet around purpose bred further questions: What was the relationship of the people I observed—those who left the meeting holding their personalized certificates in their hands—to the institutions whose imprimatur appeared on those certificates? To the exam? To each other? And finally, what imagination of "real" English would eventually animate the reform? Such questions were not simply my own but constituted the substance of the meeting, one less about how the team *should* reform the maturita and more about whether they *could* reform the maturita.

Retrospectively, I came to understand the plethora of signatures and logos on my certificate as symbolic of the trade-offs Slovakia faced as it went about "buying into English" with little money of its own to put on the table. The reform team had to juggle various entities and play their recalcitrant Ministry off the British Council, all the while balancing their own desires to raise the bar for English instruction and achieve personal recognition as the cream of an ever-proliferating crop of purveyors of English language knowledge. The "real life" of English in postcommunist Slovakia, it seemed, would be lived in negotiations and trade-offs. In the space remaining between the rocks and hard places the team encountered, they had little room to maneuver, although they persisted nonetheless. They found in the end, however, that they could not create an exam that would at once appeal to the international community and preserve the social networks they had relied upon all their lives. Because this reality was unspeakable at the level of official discourse, even as it drove virtually every moment of the meeting, what I present here is pieced together from rumors, disclaimers, denials, innuendo, and authorized documents that often seemed to draw on more of the same. As with Martina's narrative, then, there is more than one storyline to attend to in what follows.

"DOWN-TOP" RATHER THAN TOP-DOWN (THIS TIME?)

The reform team of October 2003 was almost entirely made up of current and former teachers of English, each of whom had intellectual and professional investments in the reform.[2] Aside from the foreign consultant running the meeting and me (also with our own intellectual and professional investments), eleven people were in attendance. Three were from the Ministry, including Beata—previously a secondary school teacher of English—who seemed to take a leading role. Four worked at universities as English lecturers or trainers of secondary school teachers. This category included Martina, as well as the first author of the maturita textbook, Jaroslava, who had herself previously been a secondary school teacher of English but who had become a central figure of the reform. She was often recognized by members of the reform team as a leader and was also identified by teachers I spoke to elsewhere as the state's foremost teacher trainer. Four participants were at that time currently secondary school teachers. Among this last group, three were instructors from *gymnáziá* and one from a technical secondary school.

All these participants had been actively working to improve the instruction of English in public schools since 1989. For years, as teachers during the communist regime, they had had to teach what they considered a compromised English to students who would only rarely use it. After the revolution, they relished the new materials, methods, and incentives for students that infused their courses; it seemed only natural that a new form of assessment should accompany the other changes in English language education.

There were other concerns, however, not immediately pedagogical, driving the team's efforts. The reform had galvanized the teachers beginning in the mid-1990s in part because it might offer them a chance to participate in a global economy that largely seemed to be passing them by. By 2003, the situation for public school teachers at all levels in Slovakia had gotten desperate. With accession to the European Union looming, prices had gone up dramatically, and the salaries of those who worked in the public sector had not kept pace. Teachers, because they were classified as part-time workers by the state, looked forward to lower retirement pensions than individuals filling other civil-service positions. "To have two teachers in your family is a disaster," Jaroslava remarked to me. Meanwhile, conditions at schools had not improved since the revolution, some schools struggling to cover the costs of energy, which had grown exponentially since the days of dependence on Soviet oil. Recall Maria's report in her mid-1990s letter to me that some schools had been forced to close early due to lack of funds.

Although these material conditions affected all public school teachers, English teachers faced additional threats to their status. Although nascent capitalism had brought great demand for English instruction to Slovakia, it had paradoxically undermined those very people who had made their living teaching English under the previous system. The teachers I met were furious that whereas other postcommunist states had invested directly in their English teachers after 1989—for example, sending them on trips to Britain so they could improve their skills—Slovak teachers of English had taken such trips at their own expense and had not been rewarded with any salary adjustment or recognition upon their return. The government did fund two-year programs to recertify the then-moribund Russian teachers as English teachers. But however charitable the policy of recertifying Russian teachers may have been (it kept thousands of teachers from certain unemployment), it was nonetheless a slap in the face for English teachers, suggesting that their expertise could be duplicated with only a couple of years of effort. The English teachers I met also felt that teaching skills varied widely among British and American lecturers who had been sent from abroad, and they worried about standards slipping.[3] Meanwhile the market-driven economy had made it increasingly difficult to attract the most qualified Slovak speakers of English into the profession. Working for the public school system had become one of the least profitable uses one could make of one's English language skills; one of the reform team members who had risen to become a dean at her university said she could make more money taking in private students "in my home, in my slippers." Older and more entrenched than Iveta or Viola, and facing a job market in which ageism was rampant, women like the dean were not as willing or able to entertain full abandonment of their established positions to become flexible labor—although some certainly moonlighted when possible to augment their incomes.

That the Slovak government had approved a salary raise for all teachers as part of preparations for EU accession struck the members of the reform team as insufficient. Distributed equally to all teachers (including continuing Russian teachers), the raise did nothing to honor the English teachers' crucial role in instructing future citizens how to communicate in the new lingua franca, nor did the raise recognize merit. The teachers viewed the universal raise as out of step with the logic of market economics and more in tune with the familiar ordering of favors along the lines of political loyalty. While they certainly hoped to create an exam that would benefit their students and their subject by encouraging a higher standard of instruction, they also hoped that one outcome of the higher standard would be improvement of their own beleaguered positions.

The maturita would have to go through many alchemical transformations, however, if it was to become the water that would raise all the reform team members' boats. It would have to become a force to be reckoned with. Hitherto, Slovaks had widely regarded the exam as subjective and devoid of consequences. Decentralized, its content and assessment varied from school to school, but with this consistency: virtually no one failed it. Traditionally teachers had designed the test for their own students, delivered it to their own students, and then judged the performance. Because university-bound students had to take entrance exams after secondary school graduation, the maturita, on which no placements rested, functioned more as a social ritual than as a certification or ranking mechanism. Furthermore, the old maturita, essentially an oral recitation, was designed to account for the impossibility of using English in any "real-life" context: students would frequently prepare by studying a number of stock topics such as food, culture, and geography and would often deliver a memorized speech on exam day. The reform team members hoped particularly to avoid such artificial recitation in the newly revised exam.

Although everyone was aware that the old maturita was subjective and inconsequential, the populace in general was comfortable with it precisely because it was subjective and inconsequential. The prospect of a reform that would inculcate some form of standardization throughout the country therefore provoked great unease. Many teachers, school directors, parents, and students, poised in 2003 to see the new exam go into effect in a couple of years, still weren't sure what to expect or how to prepare for it. One English teacher in a technical secondary school complained to me about the incoherence, as she saw it, of the reform-in-progress: "Nobody hated the communists more than me, but at least when they put through an educational reform in the 1980s, they knew what they were doing!" The principal of this same technical school told me she worried that the purpose of the reform was to identify some schools as less equal than others, which would have the effect of stigmatizing technical schools that had not historically specialized in languages other than Russian. Teachers worried that the inclusion of outsiders in the evaluation process would mean that their own efficacy might be questioned based on student performance. They feared that they might wind up, via the ranking mechanism of the reformed maturita, at the bottom of a suddenly stratified pile.

With opposition coming from many quarters, then, the reform of the maturita was not an easy sell. The Ministry engaged in periodic public relations work to convince the public of the benefits of the reform. In a document entitled "The Value of the Maturita Exams Today and Tomorrow; or, 'So You Won't Have to Be Tested Twice,'" the Ministry assured the populace that the new exam would retain the heritage of "our culture" embodied in the old exam, including the personal connection between a teacher and his or her student; the document nevertheless argued that the reform was necessary to create objective assessments of knowledge that would have currency in the European Union, certifying it to the satisfaction of universities and future employers.[4] Ideally, the Ministry offered, the maturita exams could replace the university entrance exams, with the big selling point that, as a result, a student would not have to be tested on the same knowledge twice in the transition from secondary to higher education.

It was a great blow, then, that 2,714 of the first high school seniors to take the new maturita exam in April 2005 had to repeat the required math maturita because one school had accidentally passed out seventy-seven exams with the answers included. Students took to the streets in mass protest. They called for the head of Minister of Education Martin Fronc, winning enough popular support that there was a vote on Fronc's recall at the legislative level. When the students sat again for the exam, some wore tee shirts emblazoned with a photo of Fronc set within the international symbol of negation: a red circle with a red line running through it. Aside from the math exam debacle, errors were discovered in the grading keys for the required foreign-language written exam, and new keys had to be circulated for evaluators of the English and German tests. In 2006, the second year of the new maturita (administered under a new minister of education), more crises emerged: Students had discovered ways to send the exam questions over cell phones or via the Internet to friends who had yet to take the exam. Some students taking the English maturita protested that the lower-level writing task, a formal letter to the European Union in which the student had to argue for the inclusion of his or her school in the European project, was actually harder than the upper-level assignment, an essay on the influence of television and media upon lifestyle.[5] Apparently it was easier for students to write about the modern media than to wrap their heads around how to appeal to the European Union on behalf of their (in many places) financially struggling schools.

I do not recall these events to suggest that the reform was a failure. Indeed, in terms of accomplishing its stated goal of gaining recognition from domestic and international universities, the reform was a success. By 2006, numerous universities both within Slovakia and abroad had begun to consider the exam's results indicative of a student's abilities. It's also worth noting that the maturita crises of 2006 occurred in Slovakia at the same time as thousands of SAT exams in the United States were improperly scored, causing disruption to university admissions nationally. The imperfections of information are writ large in the standardized testing industry, no matter the country. Neither the success nor the failure of the maturita is the point of this chapter, then, nor is the point to compare the maturita with established Western models of national tests. Rather, I would like to highlight the incomparability of the process of mass national testing in the West with the process of developing such tests in Slovakia. Administrators of the SAT or the Cambridge tests of English do not confront the considerable financial and social barriers faced by the reform team attempting to rewrite the maturita in English in Slovakia.

Further, the processes of administrating tests in Slovakia and in the West cannot be compared on the basis of efficacy because they are linked.

Consider, for example, that any blame for failures related to the administration of the maturita exams might be assigned to the British Council as much as to the Ministry, given that the British Council had been since 1997 the main financier of the reform. Once again I must note that although it might initially seem counterintuitive for the British Council to provide financial assistance to develop an exam that might engender competition with its own exam-preparation courses, the British Council was nevertheless acting in its own best interests. Sponsorship benefits sponsors and the sponsored alike.[6] The British Council was not creating competition so much as ensuring a future market. As Fero and Iveta noted, the British Council had by the millennium established a foothold in the business English market, designing courses marketed to corporations or their employees. Because English in Slovakia was a "never-ending story," even after Slovaks graduated high school with their maturitas, they would still have to seek the refined special-purpose English courses that agencies like the British Council provided. Sponsorship of the maturita also allowed the British Council to influence the intellectual direction of the reform without taking responsibility for failures that might occur (and indeed, they were not the focus of public wrath for the problems of the 2005 and 2006 exams). In short, because the British Council could presume authority and secure a somewhat proprietary relationship to the exam, it became another space the reform team had to negotiate.

The reform team nonetheless had reasons even apart from lack of funding to seek outside sponsorship. They needed a force to push against their own minister of education, who was more concerned, many suspected, with promoting religious instruction in the schools than with promoting English instruction. But pushing only worked so far. By 2003, the team's enthusiasm for the reform had been dampened by a Ministry that had not, in the reform team's view, invested enough political will to support the kind of administrative structure necessary to carry off a centrally standardized and valid exam. According to the Ministry's plan, the teachers were to be the hodgepodge administrative structure. What had started as a seeming grassroots endeavor (as Martina phrased it to me, "down-top" rather than top-down—"this time") had begun to look disturbingly like an unfunded mandate that threatened to burden already underpaid teachers with more work for no professional payoff.

There were still further hidden costs to the reform, less tangible and thus less openly acknowledged. Although the team had with great hope set about to create an exam to test English that had a "real life," a real use in the world they were joining, what they found was that global English's real life was about ranking and sorting—not only of their students but also of themselves. The 2003 meeting of the reform team took place just as the social and economic costs of capitalist integration were hitting team members, and their discussions provided a reality check to their situation: bribery would persist, administrators home and abroad would deny responsibility, their students would join the global economy as low-wage workers from whom only an "average" English would be demanded, and professional recognition would entail leaving peers behind.

AN UNSETTLING RUMOR

I was told many times that in Slovakia, getting things done is all a matter of who you know. During the communist regime, social networks served as the basis for an unofficial economy, helping people to acquire goods and information unattainable through official channels of supply. Later, after the country's economic rules had been quickly revised, the person able to maintain the broadest social networks often proved the most successful survivor of the transition. In 2003, these unofficial social networks continued to be powerful movers of information. Not surprisingly, then, much of the action when the reform team met seemed to take place in side conversations that involved exchanges of who-knew-what.

For the first breakfast of the first day, I joined Martina and Daniela, a *gymnázium* teacher and examiner for the Cambridge English certificates, as they discussed the outcomes of their last meeting to develop the writing test. Although the former exam might have been described to the public as too subjective, over breakfast Daniela put it more baldly: the former exam was corrupt. If the maturita was to someday stand in for university entrance exams, it needed to be more reliably evaluated, she maintained. It didn't matter that those entrance exams for very competitive slots at universities were themselves generally regarded as corrupt. (A recent scandal involving a dean at Komenius University's regrading of written entrance exams to improve the scores of children of friends was on the minds of many of the reform team.) The hope was that a reform of the maturita would interrupt corruption in the education system overall. To stymie corruption, the reform team had imagined that the exams would have to be evaluated at a central location under the control of the Ministry. As it turned out, however, the Ministry had decided instead that the written results of the exam would only be switched to another school for grading. Daniela said she was quite skeptical that this plan would work. Slovakia is too small, she argued. If someone knew that their nephew was at such-and-such other school, then they would do anything to persuade or bribe the teacher at said other school. Martina agreed that this was a possibility: "Everyone is for justice and against corruption—unless it's his own relation."[7]

Although the rumored plan to switch schools for grading was worrisome, far more unsettling was a detail that Daniela had heard but Martina had not: that teachers would not be paid any extra money to grade the written exam and, further, that teachers themselves would be asked to design and submit multiple prompts (or questions) to contribute to exam creation. If a teacher had seventy-five students, for example, that teacher might be asked to make up eighty-five sets of prompts—for no compensation. The prompts would be collected and retained at a central bank at the Ministry but reviewed by only one person, who would then select the prompts to appear on the final exam. Daniela felt that this proposed administrative structure placed a ridiculous and unnecessary burden on teachers; "the Cambridge," she pointed out, had a huge central administration to organize and create its tests. If the process were to ensure lack of corruption, Daniela contended, more than one person needed to be making the decisions at the top.

The "rumor" that teachers would not only have to grade the exams but write them as well was brought up immediately at the start of the first official session. Teachers who had caught wind of the news joined Daniela in complaint. The last thing they wanted was for the reform to add to the burdens of already financially strapped English teachers and schools. Another *gymnázium* teacher, the oldest of the retinue and one who had devoted a great deal of time and energy to the reform, bemoaned the reluctance of Ministry officials, fellow teachers, parents, and students to accept anything but the most surface of reforms. She worried that teachers would be particularly unwilling to witness students failing where previously almost everyone had passed. "I have been a teacher for thirty-two years," she bellowed. "I have survived many reforms!"

The consultant hired to lead the meeting acknowledged the reform team's concerns, placing some of them in the context of national exam reforms she had witnessed elsewhere. Nevertheless, she followed this acknowledgment by suggesting that the reform team not get bogged down by imagining all the political complications, economic complications, cultural complications, and the objections of all other factions (other language teachers, ministries, etc.)—that the reform team temporarily suspend all its concerns about the forces that stood in the way of change and for just a few days concentrate on the task at hand in the hopes that the process could be influenced. In a sense, the consultant wanted to bracket the reality the teachers faced in order to get the exam written. She told them that she thought of them as a think tank and handed out the schedule: Monday would be spent discussing the criteria for testing speaking and creating the scales for assessment. Tuesday would be spent creating the prompts for the exam. Wednesday would be spent reviewing the prompts and trying out several models of exams with student volunteers from a Bratislava *gymnázium,* and on Thursday, the last day, they would all evaluate their work and plan for the future. On top of the schedule, the meeting's aim was defined as designing and refining the speaking test.

For the next three days, the team attempted to stick to this schedule and embrace this aim, putting aside all the qualms they had voiced in the opening session. Real life, however, continued to intrude, disrupting the process. For one thing, the "rumor" had produced some concerns about how the meeting should proceed. If the tasks were to be written by teachers, what was the team to write? If in the end one person would decide which prompts would be included on the final exam, what was the purpose of group discussion? Given the new information about the administration of the exam, the consultant asked a specific question of the group: had examples of prompts already been devised for teachers to refer to as models? It was conceded by some members of the team that there "might" be material in draft form out there already pertaining to the speaking exam; this material, however, had not been brought to the meeting. The consultant requested that it be delivered to the meeting site from the Ministry. Because no Internet connection was available on-site, that material would be brought later by a brother of one of the Ministry representatives on the team.

These seemingly procedural moments of confusion spoke to the larger confusion of leadership at the heart of the reform process. Jaroslava, one of the authors of the textbook that I had brought to the interview with Martina, was present during the discussion of what material might already have been written without the input of the rest of the team. She worked hard not to represent herself as the author of the model tasks, although she in all likelihood was. A kind of game played out in which the consultant, who surmised that Jaroslava was effectively in charge of determining the content of the exam, would request general information about what had already been decided or devised, and Jaroslava would suggest what she had heard might be in the works.

When questions about what had been accomplished prior to the meeting and what might be expected in the future arose, members of the reform team also cast their gazes toward Beata and Vera, two representatives from the Ministry. Beata in particular was singled out as someone to press the reform team's concerns to the higher-ups, because she had been a secondary school English teacher and an active member of the association for English teachers before she joined the Ministry. But Vera and Beata were as uneager as Jaroslava to assume the mantle of responsibility; they too suggested that their hands were tied. When Martina asked if there was still time for the team to influence the direction of the speaking exam, turning toward Beata, Beata responded, "Sometimes it doesn't depend on us." She said, for example, that the mathematical formula for the assessment of all the maturita exams had been predetermined by one of their superiors at the Ministry and could not be changed. "It's his baby," Vera added. These comments indicated that this reform was no longer a grassroots endeavor; like previous reforms, it would have to be "survived." But these comments also revealed that the reform team had been divided into people who were in the know and people who were not.

Jaroslava and Beata, while clearly more informed than many others about the future of the reform, were no less frustrated by its course. Ideally, Beata argued, the reform team should be seen as the reform's advisory board. She also considered the team a think tank and hoped it stood a chance of being effective in influencing the Ministry in that capacity.

Jaroslava, on the other hand, had become thoroughly disgusted with the minister of education's actions. She was adamantly opposed to the Ministry's decision to have the exam developed and graded by uncompensated teachers, but she was pessimistic that anything could be changed. Beata countered the naysayers, pointing out that English teachers had always been on the vanguard of the reforms, had always been the vehicles for international ideas to make their way into Slovakia: "If we don't change things," she asked, "who will?"

THE HAND THAT FEEDS

Beata's question was more than merely rhetorical, but it nevertheless hung in the air as unanswerable. The people on the reform team had long wanted to "change things" in English education in Slovakia, but they knew from experience that they couldn't influence their conservative and impecunious Ministry alone. If support and funding for the maturita reform were forthcoming, the source would have to be a familiar one. As previous chapters have indicated, the British Council had ably stepped into the vacuum that was English education in Slovakia in the wake of the communist regime. Recall Fero's assertion that nothing existed on an organized basis to support teachers of English before the British Council's intervention. The members of the reform team had thus become accustomed to relying on the British Council for materials, foreign colleagues, and instructional support ever since the early 1990s (and even earlier if they happened to be in a region of the country where one of three British Council lecturers were employed during communism). The team would naturally turn to the British Council to support the reform effort.

A telling indication of the British Council's enmeshment in English education in Slovakia is revealed in the 2001 document "Agreement on Cooperation in Education and English Language Teaching and Learning." In the agreement, Slovakia's Ministry of Education and the British Council affirm that they will "support and regularly inform each other about all important activities in education in both countries for their mutual benefit. The Ministry of Education of the S[lovak] R[epublic] will inform the British Council about the development in education and training programmes and specific activities that could enhance the capacity of the British Council in support of the Ministry." Set to expire in 2004, the agreement was renewed for 2005–10.[8] This agreement evidences the asymmetrical relationship between Slovakia and the British Council: the Ministry of Education's responsibility to inform the British Council exceeds the British Council's responsibility to inform the ministry. This agreement, however, only made official a relationship already long established between the reform team and the British Council. An April 2000 press release from the British Council confirms that beginning in 1997, the council had been helping a team of English teachers, headed by Jaroslava, to reform the maturita. The press release describes the areas of the British Council's assistance: providing training bearing on the administration of the exam, the preparation of the exam, the development of materials necessary to educate language teachers, and the evaluation of the entire system.[9]

Although the reform team members looked to the British Council for sponsorship and indeed direction, they were not completely comfortable with the weight of its influence or their own dependence. Its sponsorship was more fraught for the reform team than that of the Open Society Foundation (which did little more than write checks and which was headed by Eastern European George Soros). Some on the team were ambivalent about the British Council's shifting role in English education in the country. The dean complained that the British Council used to fund lecturers who were native speakers for her university but no longer did so. She told me that when her university asked why the lecturers had stopped coming, the British Council had said, "You've had enough." But that, she pointed out, was in the 1990s, and there were new students coming to school all the time who had never had contact with "native" speakers.

More troubling, however, was the opposite problem: too much "native" English. The British Council administered the Cambridge exams, which represented to the team a powerful, and significantly foreign, model of English language assessment. As Slovakia had only existed as an independent nation since 1993, the pressure to create a Slovak exam free of any one foreign nation's influence was great. The team wanted an exam that would be recognized by the international community, but not at the expense of losing the sense of what English would mean to Slovaks entering the global economy. Martina particularly worried about replicating Cambridge exams, which she saw as related to the British Council's approach to English instruction. During our discussion in her house, she had said that while many in Slovakia saw "the Cambridge exam" as "something perfect," she saw some faults: "They [the British Council] help us, so I shouldn't be critical. But when I looked at the oral part, I liked some parts better than other parts. Personally I don't like very much describing pictures." She noted that an exam by Cambridge "is produced by native speakers, which is fine, but I think we need our own exam. . . . You see it in a different way as a nonnative speaker, knowledge of foreign language. . . . This competency of knowing idioms and figures of speech, it's not that important nowadays I think. It's an international means of communication." English for Slovaks, she felt, should not concentrate on mastery of idioms and figures of speech that in the process of international communication might simply function as noise.

The team's search for an English of "their own" affected everything from task construction to the development of instruments for assessment. The team did not, for example, consider it critical to assess pronunciation. As team members entertained the question of whether an assessment scale including the rating "exceptional" would be appropriate to Slovak students, the mood of the meeting became slightly world-weary. Anna, a teacher at a *gymnázium,* suggested, "People in Europe speak average English in general, not excellent English." She hastily offered that she was kidding, but the point that their students' most frequent conversation partners in "real-life" situations would likely be fellow Europeans clearly framed their conception of the goals of the test. English for Europeans was, Anna's comment acknowledged, only an "average" English, the median on a global hierarchy of ability. Another member of the team suggested, also half in jest, that if they wanted to design a "real-life" task their students would be conducting in the European Union, they could ask students to read a fairy tale aloud, assuming the role of au pair. It seemed from the discussion that an exam Slovaks could own would be one that acknowledged Slovakia's already defined subordinate place in the global economy. The wry laughter that followed the comments about "average" English and reading fairy tales revealed that these were not genuine suggestions of what the test should be. Each comment, rather, was redolent of black humor's mix of futility and resentment, revealing the teachers' discomfort with what their world had become.

Despite ambivalence toward the British Council, and the "not average" and "not useful" English that might be tested through Cambridge exams, it would prove impossible for the reform team to escape the influence of the British Council's English entirely. There was too much history there; some of the team had judged Cambridge exams and couldn't help but repeatedly invoke these tests as the authority on English assessment. Additionally, the team's mission to secure international recognition for the new maturita also meant that international norms for English achievement lurked in the background as models. The Council of Europe's "Common European Framework" (CEF), a structure coordinating levels of language learning across the EU, provided the framework within which the reform team had to place the maturita in order to shoot for international recognition. The CEF had been developed with the significant cooperation of the Association of Language Testers in Europe, whose membership includes major players in the language testing market—Alliance Française, Goethe Institut, and Cambridge, among other institutions—but no institution from Slovakia. To generate an exam that would be recognized in the European Union Slovakia was joining, the Slovak reform team would have to adapt to European rubrics they had no part in constructing.

In the end, however, an "average" Euro-English proved to be difficult for the reform team to embrace, simply because doing so ran counter to their own affective attachments to the English they had nurtured for so long. When a task created by half the reform team for the purpose of modeling the speaking exam was handed out for everyone's perusal, it was edited to comply specifically with British English, which had always been the standard in English textbooks, even during the communist regime. "On the weekend," for example, was corrected to "at the weekend." Anna, the one who had suggested that only an "average" English was needed, observed that "on the weekend" was "American English" and added, with apologies to me, the visiting American, "Sorry, but we prefer to use the standard." In the end, an exam of "their own" would involve elevating the English of their own, which ironically was more similar to the English of the British Council than any international or pan-European variant.

SLIGHTS AND INNUENDO

When one considers the financial, historic, and affective ties between the British Council and the maturita reform team, the following unflattering account of British national characteristics from Jaroslava's textbook, designed to prepare students for the new maturita in English, poses an interesting comment on the collaboration process: "The English are said to be taciturn, unsociable and long-suffering. The coldness may be partly due to their insularity. They have been unaccustomed to frequent social contacts with their neighbours in other countries. Due to general reluctance of the English to learn foreign languages or the violent behaviour of some British football supporters when abroad, some English people regard themselves as superior to foreigners."[10] Americans fare no better in another lesson, where they are shown to be stricken with provinciality and rudeness: "Americans are friendly and open. For other nations they seem to be noisy, dressed in colourful clothing, attracting attention. Some of their customs seem to be not very polite (e.g., putting their feet on the desk while on the telephone). They live to work because work is the most important thing in their lives."[11] This characterization of the American hard at work is a not so veiled critique of the effects of Western capitalism. Just as I heard from many Slovaks that the communist regime had encouraged people to pretend to work (the old saying "we pretended to work, and they pretended to pay us" applied here), I had heard equally often—even from the same Slovaks—that capitalism demanded an insane working schedule, with few vacations or compensated leaves for raising children. A couple of Slovak interlocutors told me that their English teachers had taught them that Americans cared about work more than they cared about their families and that Americans only made friends if doing so was advantageous. The reform team's concern about the influence of international agencies was thus not limited to concern over the British Council per se. Rather, it reflected a more general wariness about the cultural changes that had come with capitalism and a lopsided global order.

By Tuesday, the second day of the meeting, the reform team had devised the scales for assessing the exam and turned their collective attention toward creating the prompts for students. While the team was in the midst of writing the prompts, models that had already been drafted by unknown parties arrived from the Ministry. Everyone studied these drafts of the model tasks that few had known existed. These models evidenced the full influence of the Common European Framework, divided into levels corresponding to levels on the CEF. In those levels both the "average" English and the exceptional English had been inscribed. The consultant again had to negotiate the unacknowledged hierarchy in the reform team, suggesting that some other group, maybe even people present in the meeting, had filtered the CEF through the sample prompts. At this there was qualified recognition from Jaroslava.

While the reform team perused the sample prompts, the consultant asked them to read with an eye toward what factors they would consider when constructing prompts in the future. I too was looking at the sample prompts, and in a rare moment of actively participating as visiting "expert" from America, I raised the issue of cultural sensitivity: one prompt asked the test taker to compare pictures of families from different cultural backgrounds, speak about what family they would like to belong to, and speculate about the personality of one of the family members. I suggested that it might be awkward to ask students to choose a favored culturally typed family; we would avoid such questions, I opined, in multicultural America. Making this comment I fell right into a tedious performance of culturally sensitive Western observer of Eastern insensitivity. The response was swiftly offered that unlike America, Slovakia was homogeneous. Then Anna mentioned that Slovakia does include Hungarians and Romany, and upon their invocation the conversation fizzled. Jaroslava tapped the final coffin nail in the discussion by invoking the international authority of the Council of Europe (and, cannily, her own authority as the writer of the prompts): "There are certain topics not recommended by the Council of Europe, for example, violence, war, and we have avoided those."

At lunch subsequent to this discussion, I joined Jaroslava at the small table where she had eaten every day with a select group of one or two others, away from the bulk of the reform team, which tended to gather together at the big table. For a while we discussed the reasons why a professional organization of English teachers had formed in the 1990s, and then she interjected (and I don't believe as a total non sequitur) that she had had an interesting experience in America, in Scranton, Pennsylvania. She had gone to a museum of folk culture that claimed to have an old Hungarian

Bible on exhibit. She said to the tour guide, "It's not Hungarian because I can read it. It's Slovak." In another room she was presented with a Hungarian folk costume. She corrected the tour guide again, saying, "It's not Hungarian, I know the colors, and I know what region in Slovakia it is from."[12] Eventually she became so incensed by the exhibit that she asked to speak to the manager. When they brought her to the manager, the guide said, "Be careful with this one, she's a troublemaker." Jaroslava laughed loudly and launched into her next illustrative anecdote, involving a visit to another American museum, where she had encountered a list of immigrants to the United States that included one column for Czechs and one column for Bohemians. She had said to her friend who took her to the museum, "Hmm, I wonder which one am I." Her friend had replied, "I am sure you are Czech." She then mentioned that when she was in Britain she was referred to as Russian.

All these tales illustrated a common theme: the Anglophone West's ignorance of cultural and national differences in Eastern Europe. By Jaroslava's accounting, the West had failed in its basic responsibility to recognize Slovakia as a country and to distinguish Slovaks from their past occupiers and more recognized Czech neighbors. But if the West's insensitivity toward Slovaks was the rock that the reform team had to maneuver around, the persistence of the past turned out to be the hard place. Over the same lunch, the Teacher Who Had Survived Many Reforms summed up the problem with the current reform: nothing had changed in fourteen years. Beata pleaded with her to consider that change would take some time. The Teacher pishawed, contending, "Nothing has changed. Even the faces are the same. Take for example our president. For years he was a top communist. Everyone remembers what he did. Now he is a liberal democrat with *great religious convictions.* You can't believe your ears," she said. "Or your eyes," another member of the team added. There was general nodding at the table. The Teacher said the longer she was involved with the reform project, the less sure she was that the reform would work. Instead there would be enacted a "special Slovak solution" that wouldn't cost anything and wouldn't change anything.

This conversation provided a framework through which I came to understand Jaroslava's and others' criticisms of America and Britain. If nostalgia animated those criticisms, and I believe it did, it was nostalgia not for the communist past, but for a capitalism that never was. Missing from Slovaks' lives was an economic system that provided professional recognition and a livelihood for qualified, deserving English teachers. Missing too was a political system that would expose former communists who had benefited from corruption when others had suffered. Jaroslava's book ends with a polemical essay for others to emulate: a sample student-written five-paragraph theme highlighting disappointment at the outcomes of the revolution. The essay begins with rhetorical questions: "It's freedom? Can we say that we are free, when we don't have a job?"[13] This sample essay questioning the Western definition of "freedom" conveyed a combative stance toward the new economic order. The essay form, however, was fashioned on the model of the writing genre favored by the American standardized testing industry: an introduction beginning with a question, followed by three paragraphs illuminating the essay's "points," and then a conclusion. The five-paragraph theme was hardly an indigenous form in Slovakia—even in America it has no "real life" outside of school-mandated writing. On the train back to Bratislava, Anna asked me, "Why only three points?" Disappointing again in my role as the American academic expert, I couldn't say.

TESTING THE FAMOUS MAN'S SON

Late into the night on Tuesday, the team worked to prepare for modeling the speaking exam with the volunteering students from Anna's *gymnázium,* who would serve as guinea pigs the following afternoon. The consultant had divided the team into three groups; each group would test one of the three students on the set of prompts they had devised. Each group had also designed the layout of the testing site: where the student would sit, where the examiner/interlocutor would sit, and where the other judges would sit.

On Wednesday, with the students present, the tension level of the reform team mounted considerably. Each of the three mock examinations was video-recorded for review on Thursday, so the team could determine whether the judges had been able achieve some consistency in applying the evaluation rubrics they had designed. One of the mock examinations, however, fell apart so completely that it generated immediate reflection.

Surprisingly, since we could hear the student in question loudly chatting in the prep room while others were being examined, when he himself came in for the "exam," he was all but inaudible. No one could hear what he had to say about the picture he had been asked to describe. While diplomatically trying not to interrupt the exam, everyone endeavored to get the boy to speak up—writing on signs, clearing throats, making amplification-like gestures. Finally Daniela, who was at that point playing the role of one of the judges, asked the boy to speak up, but still no one in the audience could hear him. The examiner/interlocutor wound up speaking more than she wanted to, just to draw more talk out of the boy in an uncomfortable twenty minutes that should have been (for purposes of standardization) limited to fifteen.

The conversation between the boy and the teacher, in everyone's view, had failed to produce an assessable result, but interestingly, it had failed to do so precisely because it had best approximated a "real-life" (albeit incredibly awkward) exchange. The tape of the exercise demonstrated this, the conversation representing such real-life contexts as a visit to a psychiatrist's office (itself a growing feature of modern life in Slovakia after 1989), in that, in the process of helping the student complete the first two tasks, which involved describing a picture and discussing healthy lifestyles, the examiner/interlocutor had asked:

"Do you like being alone?"

"Do you sleep a long time?"

"What did you do last week that you didn't have time to sleep?"

"So you gave up [going to the fitness center], you stopped going. Why?"

"Your parents don't mind that you are on the town?"

The third prompt the boy had been given, a role play in which he was to convince his "friend" to do something with him on the weekend, was particularly thorny as it placed the examiner—in this case Karmen, an attractive teacher and one of the younger members of the reform team—in the position of having to play "hard to get":

Your friend has had a busy week and would like you to give him/her some ideas for relaxing on the weekend. You may suggest any cultural activity (e.g., film, concert, exhibition) or sporting event or activity (e.g., football match, hiking, fishing). Be warned: You may need to persuade your friend.

Teacher's instructions: Reject the idea of any physical activity since you are exhausted. Ask about the details of individual activities and then make excuses because you don't really want to participate.

To fulfill her role of drawing out more talk in this dialogue, Karmen offered at one point, "I would really like to go somewhere and spend some time with you." Such a comment demonstrated that the exam, focused as it was around problem-solving and persuasion and "real-life" situations, could do too good a job of imitating real life. Witnessing the results, the consultant suggested that in exam construction, people might take into account what dialogues might be problematic in cross-gender couplings of teacher and student.

In his written feedback assessing his experience (collected only for the purposes of the meeting), the boy responded that the experience had drained him; he said he had felt that he was losing his strength during the questioning, that the whole thing had indeed been like a visit to a psychiatrist. This feedback was interpreted by several members of the reform team as "a cry for help." Others on the team, however, suggested he might have been jerking everyone around. Speculation followed about the reasons for the boy's mental state, whether depressed or angry. Quite quickly the discussion of the boy's performance during the mock examination turned into an analysis of his personal circumstances. Several of the teachers from the Bratislava area knew of his father, a famous personality in the city; they had heard that the father had divorced and remarried someone much younger, and they wondered about the impact of such an age gap on the relationship between father and son.

Considering how badly the examination had gone for the boy, the team debated whether it would be appropriate in future exams for the teacher of a given student to brief the outside evaluator on the student's background, alerting him or her to any potential problems or vulnerabilities that might affect performance. But Beata protested that for the exam to mean anything to universities either domestically or abroad, it must retain its objectivity. Here she invoked "Cambridge," suggesting that if this boy had come in for an examination for a Cambridge certificate, nobody would care if he had psychological problems. Karmen argued, "That's completely different." Beata replied, "It was, because the exam was what it was, but we want to make it different."

Here Beata quite baldly revealed that the reform of the maturita would rearrange social relationships in the country and would (contrary to the promotional promises of the Ministry) alter the culture. When Beata suggested that the social networks Karmen had called upon should no longer signify, because they wouldn't signify in a Cambridge exam, Karmen balked. She and others wanted to be able to present background information for each of the students taking the exam (e.g., this one is a little emotional, this one's had a rough year). This information was to be the social security for students who would otherwise suffer from ranking; however, like the value of the teachers' own pensions, this form of security had become a casualty of the postcommunist transition. The ability to discuss students among themselves was one of the features of the old maturita that was clearly difficult for some on the team to relinquish. Tellingly, when the groups arranged their exam environments, each group had its own idea of where the desk should go, and of how the chairs should be arranged, but all agreed there should be flowers somewhere in the setting, because there always were. The exercise could not proceed without the flowers, a symbol of cultural continuity for which no instrumental purpose need be offered and no international endorsement given.

ALIVE, ALIVE, O

On Thursday, the last day of the meeting, the illusion that the team was collectively informing the new maturita could no longer be sustained. Visits from a superior at the Ministry and the head of the British Council of Slovakia, envoys symbolizing the proverbial "rock" and "hard place" respectively, made clear the team's compromised position. The representative from the Ministry confirmed all of the reform team's worst fears about the direction of the exam and added a few more. As feared, teachers would write the prompts and send them to a central bank at the Ministry. There, one person would evaluate, edit, and organize them. The Ministry official gave out a packet including a sample prompt that teachers could use as a model before they submitted their own: a role-playing exercise requiring the student/traveler to ask the examiner/train-station clerk for information about the most advantageous train to take to a certain town. The Ministry official struck a particularly sour chord with all involved in holding up this model prompt, just the kind of banal prompt they had wanted to avoid, alienating them even further when she suggested that English, unlike her own subject, chemistry, involved only skills, not knowledge.[14]

The head of the British Council and its program director had been walking around the grounds during the visit of the Ministry official, but they joined the team over lunch. This meeting was far more casual and, on its face, far more generous. The head of the British Council asked how the efforts at reform were going. He said he was quite sure he was sitting amid the best English teachers in Slovakia, but he wondered what would happen to the reform once the responsibility for much of the exam's content and grading was given over to all the English teachers throughout the country (this comment possibly a sideways acknowledgment that many teachers in Slovakia had only spent a couple of years learning English). Although complimenting the members of the reform team and treating them as professionals, this line of conversation nonetheless had the effect of asserting the British Council's investment in the reform. That investment would be made most clear four years later when the British Council announced its new "Maturita Preparation Course." At 8,300 Slovak crowns for thirty-six hours of instruction, the course would cost the prospective maturitant almost twice as much as the analogous course advertised at Akadémia Vzdálvania, one of the oldest and best-known Slovak-run language academies.[15] The British Council, however, advertised that its course would be taught by "our native speaker."[16]

After lunch, the reform team reconvened for its last session, reserved, according to the schedule, for a discussion of "future plans." With the head of the British Council and the representative of the Ministry both safely out of earshot, Daniela pleaded with Beata to somehow change this reform. She accentuated the banality of the train-station dialogue in the Ministry materials by reading it with comic precision before exclaiming: "What is this? Christ Almighty, what does it test? And someone is going to tell me to rewrite the maturita and write twenty-five tasks like this? Never."[17] Beata asked Daniela to write a letter to the Ministry in protest, but Daniela argued in return that she wasn't the right person to do that.

Beata responded that everyone wanted change but that no one wanted to commit to doing anything to get it. After more prompting from the team, she agreed to try to talk to her superiors at the Ministry but guaranteed nothing about the outcome. It was decided that the reform team should meet again in the near future, to try to mobilize a collective response to the Ministry's decisions. However, as the workshop was quickly coming to a close, this suggestion seemed a doomed effort to take back the reform from the bureaucratic apparatus. With time running out, the consultant read the name of each member of the team and handed each a certificate, graciously shaking hands as she did so. The team members took their certificates and left quickly to pack, to get on the bus, to go to the train station crowded with travelers making their way home in preparation for All Saint's Day. The head of the British Council drove the consultant back to Bratislava by car.

There was one event during the three-day meeting, not on the schedule, that in its relative absence of stress provided an alternative model of how the reform might have gone. The night before the charged visits from the British Council head and the Ministry official, the reform team had gathered to unwind around a large candle-lit table in the manor's spacious and inviting wine cellar. Everyone drank wine and laughed about times and meetings gone by. They were, after all, old friends. In a carnivalesque way, they parodied their current circumstances; there were jokes about how they, an almost wholly female ensemble, might attract more funding from the new (male) head of the British Council. They talked to each other using their own brand of "Slenglish," combining English root words with Slovak endings—*damagujem* and *embarrassovať*. They sang the English songs they had learned and passed on to their students, including every verse of "Cockles and Mussels":

> She died of a fever
> And no one could save her,
> And that was the end of sweet Molly Malone.

They also sang Slovak folk songs and taught some Slovak expressions to the consultant, who was an eager learner. For one evening, things were "down-top" once again.

But all this happened before the certificates, designed to give the team members evidence they could show their superiors that something had been accomplished, were handed out the next day. Those certificates, with their logos, signatures, and stamps from offices both foreign and domestic, symbolized the real life of English in Slovakia in 2003. And the English of Molly Malone? Molly Malone, as the song goes, was dead.

5   The Golden Cage

While on the one hand we may want to acknowledge
the usefulness of English as a language of global
communication, we clearly also need to acknowledge
it as the language of global miscommunication, or
perhaps "dis"communication. And I do not mean
this in any trivial fashion—I am not merely talking
here of misunderstanding, but rather of the role of
English as a language that is linked to inequality,
injustice, and the prevention of communication.
—Alastair Pennycook, "Beyond Homogeny
    and Heterogeny: English as a Global and Worldly
    Language"

He ran up to me and said: "Speak English?"
    When I nodded, he stretched his hand through
the open car window.
    "Give money!" he said.
    "Why?" I asked him, not really expecting him to
understand me.
    To my astonishment, he looked at me as if
surprised by my stupidity.
    "You have, I not have," he explained seriously in
his rudimentary English.
—Slavenka Drakulič, *Café Europa: Life after
    Communism*

BRISTOL AIRPORT, DECEMBER 2003

We had picked the wrong line again, and it wasn't moving. By my fourth
month in and around Slovakia, I had learned that if I stepped in line
behind a Slovak woman attempting to go through airport passport control to a Western European country, I would be waiting a long time. In
the wake of the 1990s rise in human trafficking from and through Eastern
Europe, single Slovak women crossing borders were often assumed to be

either present or future prostitutes or undocumented domestic workers. I knew many single women who no longer even tried to apply for visas, certain they would never be allowed to travel. One I had invited to visit me in the United States simply said, "I can't go there. I'm not married." So the scene unfolding in front of me at the Bristol airport, where I had arrived to visit Peter and Alicia, who had been living in Bristol for years, had become a routine one: a lone Slovak woman reaching into her luggage for documents other travelers were never asked to produce, pressed to answer a string of questions in English from the passport agent: "Do you always come to visit this family?" "You do come here quite frequently." "You're a receptionist?" "How much holiday do you get that you can come here so often?" The woman, who had clearly gone through this routine before, answered the questions dispassionately and quietly. Regarding the scene, I recalled my former student back in Bratislava who had been deported after just such a conversation and barred from returning to Britain—"like a criminal," she reported, still outraged years later. She had been uninformed of a change in UK policy as to how many times within a period of two years one could work as an au pair. The woman in front of my husband and me was eventually waved through, although not before we were invited to switch to a moving line.

Slavenka Drakulič, writing from the standpoint of a Croatian woman with experience of many such post-1989 crossings, notes: "We believed that after 1989 we would be welcomed to an undivided Europe, that we would somehow officially become what we knew we were—that is, Europeans. Finally, we would join the others, the French, the Germans, or the Swiss. But we were wrong in nourishing that illusion. Today, the proof of our status in Europe is easy to find. It awaits us at every western border crossing."[1] Drakulič wrote those words in the mid-1990s, whereas the distressing scene I witnessed occurred in 2003; within six months, both England and Slovakia would be part of the same European Union, a transnational entity whose very raison d'être is the free movement of people, goods, services, and information and whose governing metaphor is "Europeanness," regardless of nationality. Much has been made of the fact that the lubricant for this mobility, and somewhat paradoxically the very glue allowing these transnational entities to communicate and therefore cohere as "Europeans," has become English. Less appreciated, however, is the potential for miscommunication and misinformation that English as lingua franca presents. At the same time as English has become the language of global communication, English has also become, as Alastair Pennycook has determined, the language of "'dis'communication"—a language that lets people know their place rather than move around and especially up in the global order. Pennycook notes that English has become linked to "forms of institutionalized power" (of which border controls are one example).[2] However, English has become the language of "dis"communication not simply because it represents the stability of particular powerful nations or institutions, as Pennycook suggests. Rather, English has become the language of "dis"communication because there are gains to be made by using it in artful and even illegal ways. Capitalism has made a game of English with few—if any—unbreakable rules governing how information can be withheld, distorted, or extracted. The conversation between border guard and would-be cosmopolitan citizen of new Europe was a battle over information in which there was a presupposition that distortion could occur from either side, at any point.

What has been called the utopian (some would say "triumphalist") view of English as a global language holds that all people who learn English will have equal access to the world's information that it encodes.[3] In other words, what happened to my former student—deportation due to lack of information—might not happen again once knowledge of English and information in English are generalized, with no party having the upper hand. This notion mirrors what Joseph Stiglitz calls "the Washington consensus" view of development, one, he charges, that simplistically assumes perfect information in its model for growth in developing countries. Stiglitz argues that the Washington-consensus model does not work as well for developing economies as established ones because information disparities, inherent to capitalism in practice, will always have dire consequences for those less able to buy/manipulate information.[4] As Jan suggested, the British have had the luxury of being misunderstood, because others always strive to understand them. For Slovaks communicating in English, however, the consequences of any miscommunication are often profound. As long as English remains central to the market, it will be used to create information asymmetry—and used most efficiently by those already on top; no equilibrium, in which the whole world holds a version of English perfectly in common, will therefore be reached.

Previous chapters have touched on this reality, perhaps most strongly in the portrait of Maria, who referred to English as having changed for her from "freedom" to "a new kind of slavery." Rather than opening doors for her, English had made her more and more aware of her own marginality as an Eastern European artist. For their part, Peter and Alicia, very much the transnational subjects of globalization, having made the move from Eastern to Western Europe, were nonetheless fearful that their two young daughters would be on the losing side of the asymmetries of information they saw emerging all around them. They knew that English was to be—in fact already was, despite the protests of the French—the language of the European Union.[5] "English fortunately, or unfortunately, is it," Peter declared. As English gained in global stature, Peter and Alicia's sense of how much exposure to English their children would need steadily increased.

In many ways Peter and Alicia were obvious beneficiaries of the information economy; they made their living by designing software to facilitate the intra- and international exchange of information. But their entry into this line of work, and into England, had tellingly not been smooth. Peter and Alicia had first come to England in 1997 for a brief two weeks, without their children, to work as subcontracted labor on a software project. Working around the clock for those two weeks, they perceived that the job would require a longer stay, and they went back for their daughters. Their first major project linked health databases throughout the UK; subsequently Peter began working with the European Union to do the same for all of Europe.[6] Peter's work with the EU demanded that he travel widely, for the most part back to Bratislava, where he maintained an office and where his staff remained (allowing him to maintain low overhead), but he also frequently traveled to Rome, Leiden, Brussels, and the Italian Alps to meet with EU administrators. Given the transnational nature of his work, the family could by 2003 theoretically have moved anywhere in the EU that information technology could reach. Year after year, however, they decided to stay in England, Alicia worrying that if they left, the children would forget the English they had acquired.

Even though situated at a nexus of information transfer in the EU—indeed, even though creating that nexus—Peter and Alicia, as Slovaks, nonetheless continued to feel the weight of persistent global information asymmetries. All the while Peter and Alicia lived in England, Slovakia was being vetted as a contender for foreign investment, a process that involved constant surveillance of the political, social, and economic state of the Slovak people. As Peter put it, "The West is taking Slovakia's temperature daily." The media was full of assessments of each postcommunist state and its relative progress toward economic and political reform, as defined by the European Union and other transnational entities. Information in English on Slovakia and Slovaks had proliferated along with these assessments. Peter and Alicia had become ever more acutely aware of what the West thought of Slovaks by watching English language television and reading English language newspapers (whether in the UK or in Slovakia). The cumulative message they absorbed from the media was that the West thought Slovaks were good workers but primitive people, insufficiently developed to become fully mobile subjects of capitalism. This sense was confirmed by their experiences in England and in their work with the EU, through which they were constantly reminded of their secondary place in Europe.

They also constantly rejected this assigned place. Peter and Alicia had, like many Slovaks, constructed a rebuttal to the charge of backwardness levied against them. It was the West that was backward, they argued, not Slovakia; England, which would allow Czechs—but not Slovaks—to enter without visas in 2003, was by dint of this arbitrariness the most backward place of all. Recall the passages from Jaroslava's book preparing students for the maturita that characterize the British as insular and failing to learn foreign languages—in other words, as out of step with globalization. Repeatedly I heard from Slovaks (with the notable exception of Fero) that England was slow, dirty, and mired in bureaucracy and traffic. Western Europe and America were similarly regarded as failing to keep the engines of progress humming. The West was supposedly "teaching" Eastern Europeans about capitalism, but many voiced suspicion that the rules they were being asked to follow in order to join the EU existed primarily to protect Western Europe from losing business and employment to the more flexible, hungrier East. Iveta, for example, felt that the production quotas and restrictions on labor the EU placed on Slovakia had not been created to benefit Slovakia; she was frustrated that Slovak politicians failed to stand up to the EU even when a given mandate was clearly against Slovakia's own interests.[7] Peter complained that the EU moved at the pace of a snail. The EU commission hiring him had given him eighteen months to do work that he felt he could have completed in a matter of weeks. He described Slovakia in the final months before accession as racing against a new kind of imposed immobility; the Slovak government was doing all it could to attract foreign investment in this period because after EU accession in May 2004, Slovakia, Peter claimed, "won't be able to do anything for one hundred years."

Even though Peter, Alicia, and other Slovaks refuted the discourses that marked them as backward, they nonetheless still felt trapped by them. Peter's comment about not being able to do anything for one hundred years flies in the face of the commonplace that globalization is synonymous with motion; indeed, he was just one of the many people whom I met who reported feeling stuck. Knowledge of English, supposedly the gold of the information economy, had not only failed to grant them the mobility they had sought; it had perversely added to their feelings of immobility by initiating them more forcefully into the unbalanced world. To witness this perversity of English—how it could be at once gold and a cage—we join Peter on the other side of passport control.

LIFE IN ENGLAND

Peter picked my husband and me up at the Bristol airport. It was the middle of the day, and Alicia was working in her position as "Senior Software Developer" at the agency at which she had previously been migrant labor, but Peter, as a consultant to the EU, made his own hours. He had lots of time on his hands, he said, because the EU moved so slowly. On the way back to the house, he took us zipping along his favorite back roads in his BMW. He had spent many a day exploring the countryside, looking to avoid the notoriously congested freeways of Southern England; he recounted as he drove the more spectacular jams he had braved and the bizarre behavior of English drivers who failed to negotiate even the mildest weather. But he had also explored every back road in the vicinity of his home because driving, at least temporarily, assuaged his boredom.

Cars have long been a symbol of progress in developed and capitalist countries, symbolizing freedom, wealth, and personal mobility. Accordingly, as Peter's wealth developed after the fall of the communist regime, his stable of cars grew. I have a photo of him taken in 1993 in his cramped apartment in Bratislava, when he had only two cars, a Lada (his first, state-allocated car) and an ancient Russian Volga wagon he had just bought. In the photo he balances his infant daughter with one hand on his lap while he points with his other hand to an advertisement for a Ford Explorer in a magazine. His eyes say, "I want this." He envisioned that with such a car he could get to and from his family's cottage in the hills of middle Slovakia on even the snowiest of days. By 2003 Peter owned seven cars, split between England and Slovakia: three Western models (two BMWs and a Ford Sierra for the mountains) and four of Eastern Bloc origin (the Lada, the Volga, and two ancient Tatras). And yet he lamented that after six years in England, he spent most of his time sitting in traffic. Often he sang to me the praises of Slovakia's extensive public transportation system, through which, he pointed out, you could get anywhere in the country for almost nothing in a matter of a few hours. He found England's public transportation system, in contrast, both expensive and inefficient. Alicia once waited three hours for a bus to the airport, he complained. Hearing the news that bus routes in Slovakia were being privatized and cut back, he worried that Slovakia's bus system would soon follow England's example.

But perhaps even more galling to Peter than not being able to drive anywhere in England was that he and Alicia couldn't even walk where they wanted in the country. "Every piece of England is owned" by someone, they complained, making it impossible for them to get from place to place except by the most circuitous route. For most of their lives, they had had the run of the Slovak countryside, sleeping outside in the open air when they chose, at most having only to ask at a nearby farmhouse for permission. They had hiked, biked, and skied vast stretches of the Slovak countryside without interruption, often with their huskies leading the way. In contrast to this freedom of motion, Peter and Alicia found every movement in England predetermined by footpaths, hedges, and stone fences—

the remnants of the division of the commons into private property, the landmark achievement of capitalism in practice.

Through the back roads to Bristol, then, past the patchwork of lands demarcated with hedges and walls, we arrived at their house, located in a series of interconnected planned developments known as Bradley Stoke, or, as the locals called it, "Sadly Broke." The play on the name denoted the orderly but soulless nature of this development designed to house the newly upwardly mobile. It also suggested the state of people's bank accounts after paying for homes that cost upward of 300,000 pounds. Nevertheless, after many years of renting in the area, Alicia and Peter had decided with great anxiety to buy a home, this decision a partial admission that they were not returning to Slovakia for at least a few years. The process of securing a loan as Slovaks in England before Slovakia became part of the European Union was difficult. Alicia wrote to me of her frustration with the lenders, who, when they realized that Slovaks "don't sleep on beds of roses," were hesitant to extend the mortgage. Peter and Alicia, legally foreigners and therefore bad credit risks, had to put down one quarter of the house price (nearly 100,000 pounds) in cash. When they finally did acquire the house, they worried that their grandchildren would be paying it off someday, or that they would lose substantially if they chose to return to Slovakia in a few years. Alicia's father suggested that they had bought the house at the most expensive time possible, just when the last of the British Empire had crumbled and all the British were returning home—from Hong Kong, from South Africa.

Alicia welcomed us to her "golden cage," as she called her home. Relatively opulent in comparison to the house they had left behind in Slovakia, it had two floors and two and one half bathrooms. More significantly, the house had come requiring nothing like the parade of ongoing do-it-yourself maintenance chores that were the stock-in-trade of home ownership in Slovakia. At their house outside Bratislava, for example, Peter had had to dig a trench from the street to the house before the water company would come to lay pipe. Four friends had been recruited to stand on a wooden beam to leverage the driveway stone up to a level where Peter could force boulders under it to even it out. They had had to wait for a phone. The English house, in contrast, came wired to phone lines, plumbed to water.

When Alicia referred to her "golden cage," however, she meant not only the physical house with its four walls and many rooms but also her entire life in England. To Alicia, England was a country of contradictions—lavish facilities with absurdly restrictive rules posted everywhere, making those facilities virtually unusable or, at the very least, difficult to enjoy. She was mystified by signs everywhere in England instructing the populace how to execute routine activities correctly: A sign on the mirror of a public bathroom, for example, directed visitors to shake their hands over the sink so as not to make the floor wet and therefore slippery. Another at the gym spelled out the rules for use of the hot tub. Unaccustomed to the rhetorical situation produced by an atmosphere of rampant litigation, Alicia found these signs indicative of nothing more than inherent stupidity on the part of the British populace. What mother wouldn't know how long to allow her child to sit in the hot tub? Why would you deliberately get the floor of the bathroom wet? Why did people need to be told these things? Did they have no common sense whatsoever?

Although these proscriptions had been present in England for the entire time that Alicia had lived there, they only impinged on her consciousness when she gained the ability to read them. Her competence in English over the years she lived in Britain had grown slowly because for the first two years she had been entirely surrounded by a team of Slovak software developers; like the other members of the team, she had relied on Peter's English to facilitate interactions with their British employers. When Alicia's increased knowledge of English allowed her to secure a position as an employee of the governmental agency, rather than as subcontracted labor almost entirely dependent on her husband/employer's language skills, she ironically did not feel herself to have greater freedom at work; on the contrary, her fluency in English enabled her to become part of a work culture she found counterproductive. Once a full-time employee, she now faced the rule that she must arrive in the morning and leave at four-thirty P.M.; she felt she had no incentive to work longer than the allotted time, even if she had done nothing all day but attend meetings. The result of this schedule, she complained, was that she would be all but asleep before lunch, accomplishing nothing. When she really got going, after lunch, she would be required to go home after a few hours. Once at home she would have no incentive to work because she was only paid for work in the office. This whole system, in her mind, compared quite unfavorably with when she was working from home in Slovakia, in the heady, entrepreneurial days of the mid-1990s. Then she had made her own schedule: during the day, she took care of the children; from their bedtime until three A.M., she wrote code. To her such a schedule, though short on sleep, reflected true productivity and free enterprise—what she had expected a capitalist economic system would eventually embrace and reward with greater remuneration and autonomy. It was with great disappointment, then, that she faced the opposite when she moved to England. She grated at having "face time" priced minute by minute and seemingly at a higher rate than the products of her ingenuity. She found the formalities of the position immobilized not just her but the progress of the agency: "Everything is slowing down now, and the only important thing is the rules. Not important is that you work, only important is that you are there."

"THEY THINK WE COME FROM BANANA TREES"
Peter and Alicia's analysis of England's failure to keep up with the pace of globalization was defensive at its core. In the 1990s, Slovak/British relations had become increasingly fraught, particularly due to the British institution of a visa requirement in 1998 for all Slovaks seeking to enter or transit the country. Slovaks resented the visa requirement greatly, seeing it as a signifier of their second-class status. Even those Slovaks who could afford to pay for a visa were so put off by the requirement's very existence that they refused to apply. Goran, for example, Peter and Alicia's near-lifelong friend, told me that he would never visit them in England while the visa requirement remained in place. On December 8, 2003, Britain announced the cancellation of the visa requirement for Slovaks before the year's end. I was with Peter and Alicia in Bristol when they heard the news on the Slovak channel they watched through their satellite system. They were thrilled, foreseeing an end to the hassle and humiliation of having to acquire visas, and realized that Peter's brother's family could visit after the holidays without having to pay. (As it turned out, when the extended family did visit the following January, they still faced a great deal of trouble at the border for not having the correct paperwork.) Goran, in Slovakia, text-messaged "Prepare the beds" to their phone in Britain as the news came over the station they were all watching simultaneously.

The visa requirement was mostly resented for its ostensible and much-publicized goal: preventing the immigration of Romany asylum seekers to England that had begun after the fall of the Berlin Wall. The British felt Romany asylum seekers were taking advantage of their relatively open so-cial-welfare policies in numbers too large to support and looked to the visa requirement to stem the perceived tide. It seemed unreasonable to many Slovaks that everyone in Slovakia should be punished for the actions of a minority, particularly a minority that the dominant group rejected as cul-turally deprived and therefore unrepresentative of Slovak citizenry. But Slovaks also felt that the visa requirement revealed hypocrisy at the heart of the European Union. One of the mandates Slovakia had been required to satisfy before being admitted into the European Union was an upgrade of its antidiscrimination legislation. The West had identified the Roma as one group particularly in need of protection in Eastern Europe. Indeed, the position of the Roma in Slovakia was economically and socially dire; they were (and still are) widely despised by the majority, in many regions unassimilated into the mainstream. From the Slovak point of view, how-ever, while the British wanted fair treatment of the Roma in Slovakia, they were unwilling to provide a home for them on their own soil. This dis-agreement over the Roma took place within the context of larger debates over globalization, the role of the EU, and the control and circulation of information. Millennial Europeans in both the West and the East had be-come leery of the power the European Union had assumed. That power, exercised politically and economically rather than militarily, was largely dependent upon English, as the following critical incident reveals.

On September 8, 2003, a story appeared in Slovakia's only English language weekly, the *Slovak Spectator,* reporting the paper's discovery of offensive jokes about the Roma told in Slovak on a humor Web site hosted by the Slovak arm of the British mobile telecommunications company Or-ange.[8] Although customers had posted some of the jokes, they had been at least tacitly invited to do so by Orange's database, which had provided a category for jokes entitled "Gypsies and Roma."[9] The *Slovak Spectator* re-ported that Orange had responded to the paper's inquiries about the jokes by removing both the jokes and the category from the Web site. Although the *Slovak Spectator* presented the story as part of an exposé on the preva-lence of anti-Roma humor in Slovak society, the paper's translation and publication in English of a sample of the jokes—many of them relying on the death or dismemberment of Romany people as the source of their "humor"—drew sharp criticism from the English speaking readership of the newspaper's online edition. A week after the story's appearance, the editorial board of the *Slovak Spectator* responded to audience pressure by removing the jokes from the paper's online edition.

Somewhat serendipitously, I had interviewed the author of the story the day it ran in the paper but before the controversy with the readership erupted. The author, a young Slovak law student who had spent a year of his secondary school education in Iowa, was one of the *Slovak Spectator*'s small cadre of full-time reporters (by 2003, most of the staff were Slovaks writing in English because many of the British and American nationals who had for years comprised the bulk of the paper's staff had changed jobs, moved farther East, or gone home). I asked him if he had experienced censorship in his position; he said that he didn't feel that he was subject to it. He picked up the current edition of the paper and showed me the story he had written about the jokes, pointing out that he felt free to write about Orange, even though Orange was one of the *Slovak Spectator*'s leading advertisers. Interestingly, he imagined that the call for censorship would come from the corporate world, if it came from anywhere at all (not a surprising conclusion, as the *Slovak Spectator* devoted a sizable portion of its news to business developments within the country and printed special publications and guides for foreign investors; the reliance on corporate advertisers was such that the paper's online archive of past articles had been at times visibly sponsored by corporate entities as varied as the consulting firm KPMG and the now-defunct Russian oil company Yukos).

When I contacted the author after the uproar from the readership and the subsequent editorial decision to delete the jokes from the online edition of his story, he admitted to me that this was the first time in his experience that a call to pull some of the paper's material had been answered, and he was quite surprised by the origin of the call. He said he wondered how many of the paper's concerned readers had taken Orange to task for hosting the database. This statement enunciated the frustration that a Slovak-run (albeit American-owned) publication—in this case the *Slovak Spectator*—had been accused of discrimination, while the Western agency that sponsored the discrimination—in this case the company Orange—escaped without rebuke from Western readers, as far as he knew.

Following the publication of the story, an online discussion in English among readers debated the paper's culpability for reprinting the story on the anti-Roma jokes. This discussion further evidenced the tensions between the international, largely Western human rights community and Slovakia. A Dutch human rights worker weighed in, authoritatively: "A description of the jokes would have been enough. I work for the Dutch Complaints Bureau for Discrimination on Internet . . . and we deal with discriminatory content on a daily basis. Our main aim is to get material removed, while Orange did the right think [sic] by removing the material, the Slovak Spectator put it back on line. A while back you had an article about a extremist site who had a hitlist and you put the URL on line, same thing there, people who didn't know about it or had lost the link (they had moved 3 times pending a criminal investigation) could find the hitlist through your website. Not a good idea."[10] The Dutch human rights worker's posting received a response from a Slovak reader of the paper, questioning the human rights worker's jurisdiction and her interest in the incident: "Mind if I ask how come that you, as an employee of the Complaints Bureau in Holland, i.e. serving the Dutch community, also visits a site such as this one? Does this mean that checking Slovak sites is part of your job description? If so, is that considered necessary? The world is a big place; it seems a bit odd that you spend some of your time reading (uitgerekend) Slovak material." Yet another comment from the same reader immediately followed this post. He reported that he was at that moment watching a Dutch TV program about referenda for the European Union constitution. He complained that the footage illustrating the program's point that referenda are common in Eastern Europe showed only Roma at a Slovak voting place. Citing this image as unrelated to the program's content, he charged that the program was deliberately manipulating the Dutch perception of Eastern Europe: "It makes the Dutch public think that Slovakia (fortunately most Hollanders won't recognise the Slovak flag) is filled with poor Roma. It now only takes a skinhead in Slovakia to bang a Roma over the head, and 'Nova' has another juicy story. This is either plain laziness, or a playing on the subconsious of the Dutch public. You don't have to answer, but I hope you saw it too, and that you realise that, although your job may be noble, Dutch involvement in Eastern European problems should not be just someone like you telling the Slovaks what you think from your single-sided perspective." Significantly, this post invoked an early battle over the European Union's Constitution, perhaps the most contentious EU issue of 2003 (becoming in 2005 an issue that threatened the EU's coherence when the Dutch, following the French, rejected the constitution in referenda). The Slovak writer charged that the Roma were being used as pawns in a bid to eclipse Slovak national sovereignty. As the discussion thread continued, strong lines of demarcation emerged in which the Westerners (many of them first-language speakers of English) invoked human rights issues and the Slovaks (speaking English as a second language) invoked the West's hypocrisy.

What is clear is that had the original article been written in Slovak instead of English, the article would have gone unnoticed; the call for the removal of the jokes would likely not have occurred, nor would the ensuing international discussion about the incident. Few people in the Netherlands speak Slovak, and few in Slovakia speak Dutch. Yet although the discussion among the readership took place in English, English did not place everyone on an entirely equal footing. Later on in the discussion thread, a Slovak reader challenged one of the first-language Anglophone readers to produce "one simple sentence" in Slovak, in order to establish his credibility to speak on the issue. This reader attempted to change the language of the debate, the authority of the debaters, and indeed the general global tide by labeling knowledge of English inadequate to understand the complexity of Slovakia's position.[11]

Slovaks had good cause to be concerned that the attention to the Roma emanating from the established countries of the EU was not entirely altruistic. Independent reporters from the United Kingdom whom I interviewed in Bratislava confirmed (speaking under condition of anonymity) that the British press had gone out of its way to whip up fear of a Romany invasion in Britain, scouring the Slovak countryside for scare stories of migrating Roma after it was announced that the visa requirement would be lifted. When the wave of Roma did not materialize, the media sought to invent one, an outlet in one case even asking a reporter to pay Roma to go to the airport and stand in line so they could be photographed (this reporter declined). The stories that were printed, however, were so rabid in their xenophobia that Denis MacShane, Britain's Europe minister, was moved to decry the "rancid hate campaigns" launched by the tabloids against the new Eastern European members of the EU.[12] However, even when the British tabloids' smear campaign was exposed, as it was in the *Economist*, in an article that noted the flood of British journalists into eastern Slovakia, the coverage reinforced the notion of the Roma as a problem. The *Economist*'s February 2004 article entitled "Those Roamin' Roma," for example, featured a photo of a Romany family standing outside their dilapidated house, with the caption "Have freedom of movement, will travel."[13]

It was in December 2003, not long before the "Roamin' Roma" article appeared, that I conveyed to Peter and Alicia what the journalists had told me about being asked to pay Roma to pose at the airport. They immediately launched into their honed critique of the Western media. Knowledge of English had put Peter and Alicia in a position from which they could understand Western media portrayals of Slovakia; however, it had not placed them in control of those portrayals. Alicia told me that now that she could read in English, she was disturbed by the images she saw of Slovakia in the Western press: "You would think that all Slovaks were poor and living in dirt."[14] For Peter and Alicia, these media distortions were quite consequential in terms of their own physical and economic mobility, since British immigration policy had treated all Slovaks as a potential drain on Britain's resources. As of October 2003, Peter still had to pay 15,000 crowns (then roughly 500 dollars) for visas for himself and his family to continue to work in Britain, despite the fact that he was at that time working for the European Union. The more Peter worked in Western Europe, the more he became convinced that he, as a Slovak, would be saddled with second-class status in the new Europe. He recalled to me that his first bid to win the contract to create a network and database linking health systems across all EU countries had initially been met with the news that his firm's location in Slovakia rendered it ineligible, even though by the end of the project Slovakia would be in the EU. "They tried to get rid of me," he remarked. Peter had had to establish a corporate presence in England at some expense in order to win the contract. Peter bemoaned his dealings with the EU: "They think we come from banana trees."

Peter offered up a particular example of how the West's distorted perception of Eastern Europeans complicated his attempts to conduct work in English. His firm supported one system that, although centralized in

Brussels, served many European countries. His staff routinely fielded questions via email from many of the satellite countries, working with those countries to resolve problems. The most common medium for these communications was, of course, English. Once, a member of Peter's staff wrote to one Scandinavian site that he was "exhausted" from working on their problem and would get to it later. Peter, copied on the email, immediately recognized a critical misuse of the word "exhausted." The client in Scandinavia took offense and wanted to cancel the system. Peter had to explain to the central organization in Brussels that what had occurred was a miscommunication due to his employee's limited command of English: "You know this guy," he told them. "He is very polite. Even if he were exasperated" (as Peter conceded to me he probably was at that point) "he wouldn't say it." The team member told Peter he had meant to say that he was working hard on the problem and would get back to them later.

Peter's story of the near loss of a contract due to a misuse of a delicate phrase in English prompted me to recall another conversation Peter and I had about his work in 1994, and here I warn that I am working from memory. I was in Peter and Alicia's house, before it had a phone and before it had water. Peter had nevertheless taken a break from the digging to work on posters for an upcoming conference in Amsterdam where he would display the software he and Alicia had been developing. He asked me to look over the English and correct it, which I did, joking that I should stay in Slovakia and open an editing business. Peter said quite seriously that he had just been thinking that I could do that. But then he cast a weary eye around his house and reconsidered. Slovaks, he felt, needed things like phones before they needed to know the difference between "that" and "which."

What Peter's team member had failed to do was not really on the order of grammatical correctness. He had rather failed to perform a routine expression of business parlance that would indicate inexhaustible attentiveness yet defer any actual action until a convenient time. Because he didn't have such a phrase in his repertoire, he had tried to construct one on the fly and run afoul of the implications of "exhausted" in the business setting. The fallout from such miscommunications frustrated Peter not only because it slowed him down but also because it added to the Western perception of Slovak companies' unfitness for commerce. Pleading his firm's case, like applying for visas, was yet one more humiliation. "And this," he sighed, "is what I spend my time doing."

Failure to perform business parlance might have been the cause of the initial communication error; however, the resulting near cancellation of the service suggests the work of "'dis'communication" in maintaining hierarchies of the global order. The West perceived that the customer service skills of Eastern European firms were deficient or perhaps even irremediable, due to decades of communism, during which customers were not pandered to at all. The email sent by Peter's team member confirmed this impression by failing to perform the cheerful obsequiousness that is the ideal of capitalist customer service, never mind that in most economically developed countries of the West, cheerful obsequiousness is only performed perfectly (and endlessly) by prerecorded messages.

The result of Peter's disaffection with the EU was a sense of bafflement. The work he had done for Western Europe, and his constant negotiations of European bureaucracy, had made him feel that he had earned a place there. Accordingly, he filled out an application to take the test to become a European Union administrator. He professed not to want to be an administrator (the salary incentive of thousands of euro per month— a considerable draw for many Slovaks—was not an object for him), but he said he hoped to find out through the selection process "what they are looking for. If not me, then who?" Who, he wondered, would the EU embrace, if not someone who had already been working within EU administration for several years, even though his English, as he described it, was "only average"? As it happened, Peter's application, perhaps due to some glitch in the online submission process, never did get completed, so he was not in a position to take the application exam. Nevertheless, in stark contrast to his view in 1994 that meticulous English was of no great economic consequence, it is telling that in 2003 he saw his Achilles heel as his "only average" English. He had learned from experience that "only average" English was not something a Slovak could afford. He and Alicia both felt that to prepare for the EU, their children's English must be far better than average. It must be as fluent as the Scandinavians' English, if not superior. It must be so good that the daughters might not be seen as Eastern European at all.

DIRTY ENGLISH

As the exchange over the Orange jokes demonstrates, Slovaks did not take the Western representation of them as unsuitable for full European Union citizenship lying down. Marked in the English language media as filthy and destitute through the circulation of images of the poorest Roma, regarded as generally unable to master the verbal cadences of the global economy, they heaved the worst of these charges back at their most vocal accusers—the British. The Brits were not simply self-interested, Slovaks maintained, not even merely hypocritical, but actually dirty, hapless at those basic domestic tasks whose execution forms the bedrock of civilization. The stories they told about the British, while circulating at a much more informal level than British stories about the Slovaks, could be just as hyperbolic. More than once, Jan told me of a waiter in England who had served him a sandwich while wearing a disgustingly filthy shirt. Jan reported that he had refused to eat the sandwich, had confronted the waiter, and had threatened to punch him for his offense. He further revealed that a Slovak woman who had worked as an au pair in England had told him that the mother of her employing family would go straight from using the toilet to preparing a meal without washing her hands. Indeed, it was not unusual for Slovak au pairs to return from England with stories of British mothers' failure to perform even the most routine domestic duties.[15] Peter and Alicia, living in England for years, worried about British dirt contaminating their daughters. Alicia spoke of how her children were the only ones in school who had not been sent home with lice. Working for a governmental health organization, Peter and Alicia were also aware of, and alarmed by, escalating rates of tuberculosis in Britain.

Yet if Peter and Alicia's children were going to learn English perfectly, they would have to live among those British bodies. Peter and Alicia both believed that the only way their daughters could master English would be by going to school in an Anglophone country. Alicia spoke of her father, who had learned Slovak, Czech, German, and Hungarian fluently as a child just by playing with the children in his neighborhood. Peter explained, using an expression that spoke directly to the filthy comingling of bodies, "They have to pee on the same fence together." Thus their daughters, by 2003 aged ten and eight, had spent approximately half their lives in England and spoke British English with greater facility than they spoke Slovak.

Of course, this bothered Peter. Although he had always shown a preference for the American variant of English over the British, that preference intensified as his dislike of England grew. By 2003 Peter had embarked on a program to counteract the most culturally identifiable aspects of British influence on his own and his family's English speech. He took great care to pronounce the short *a* typical of American English rather than the long *a* typical of British English and teased the children for their pronunciation of "cat." Alicia, on the contrary, embraced the accent and verbiage she was absorbing in her office. The fact that Peter worked alone from home made his program to speak an English almost devoid of Briticisms fairly easy to carry out, but with Alicia's speech he was fighting a losing battle and with his children a lost one. Both daughters had (naturally) acquired very strong British accents. Nevertheless, they too attempted not to appear too British in certain circumstances. They had picked up on the increasingly negative feelings toward Britain most Slovaks held and had become so self-conscious about being labeled British on their visits to Slovakia that they adapted their speech accordingly. Alicia observed that although the girls mixed up Slovak and English words in the same sentences continually in England, they never did so in Slovakia, where they struggled to speak Slovak exclusively.

By 2003, the daughters' acquisition of English was producing a problem more troublesome than their British accent: they were forgetting (or, in the case of the younger one, failing to acquire) Slovak. On the family's visits to Slovakia, the children were mistaken for Hungarian on the basis of their faulty Slovak. The problem, Alicia felt, was that they were forced to depend entirely on their parents to learn the language. And even though they spoke Slovak at home in England, Alicia pointed out, it was very simple Slovak that didn't regularly rehearse the declensions of all Slovak cases. The older daughter would have to know these declensions in order to pass the mandatory Slovak tests to get into a good Slovak high school. The younger daughter, who had lived more than half her life in England, had difficulty with even basic written Slovak.

Here was the vexing symmetry underlying all the asymmetries Peter and Alicia faced. They were worried that the West would regard their children as "backward" because of their English; they were also worried that their children would seem "backward" at home because of their Slovak. Peter fretted that forgetting Slovak would make the children less Slovak. Alicia too had concerns that the program to perfect the daughters' English had carried unintended side effects, making them more English. She said that when she was young, to have an orange was a great event. Having nothing, she was very happy to have an orange. Her children, she worried, had everything and so wouldn't know that kind of happiness. In fact, while Peter and Alicia could afford to send their children to any private school when they eventually returned to Bratislava, they wanted their oldest daughter to attend a traditional *gymnázium* rather than a private school designed for the children of foreigners, so that she might learn the old ways and "pee on the same fence" as other Slovak children. In 2005, still living in England, their oldest daughter completed all her homework for her British school as well as all the homework for a Slovak school so she would be able to place into *gymnázium* upon their return. (This was all home-schooling, there being no industry in Britain for teaching Slovak.) In short, the family's investment in English—not just any English, but an English they hoped could raise the children above the indignities of "dis"communication in their encounters with the West—demanded much extracurricular work, but more significantly much faith that their children would still be recognizably theirs when all was said and done.

NEXT YEAR, IN SLOVAKIA

In my mind, the last time I saw Peter and Alicia was in Slovakia, on my final night in Bratislava: December 22, 2003. They had returned to Slovakia for Christmas vacation. We had planned to meet at a restaurant off one of the main access roads to town. Peter and Alicia arrived late, having underestimated the Bratislava traffic at rush hour. They came in perplexed and flustered, remarking that they hadn't remembered there being so many cars on the road.

It takes some mental effort for me to recall that the last time I saw them was not in fact in Slovakia, but in Vienna, Austria, later on that evening. Peter, Alicia, and Peter's father very kindly drove us over the border so my husband and I could stay the night at an airport hotel and catch our early flight the next morning. I went to the front desk of the hotel to pick up our reservation and get the key, while Peter and his father helped my husband carry the bags. The moment the hotel clerk overheard Slovak speakers entering the lobby with copious luggage, his performance of cheerful obsequiousness for my benefit ended. When Peter asked me in English which room to take the bags to and headed down the hall, the hotel clerk looked panicked. He immediately informed me in English, "Only two people allowed per room."

I have not seen Peter and Alicia since that December night. Competing work schedules have made it difficult for us to meet in Slovakia, and none of us have much of an appetite for another meeting in Bristol. I suggested that they visit us in America again, as Peter and Alicia had for six weeks in 1996. Peter said this wouldn't be a bad idea, except that he would have to get a visa and thus would have to submit to questioning as if he were a terrorist, and he just couldn't see putting himself through that. I asked when they were moving back to Slovakia for good. They gave their perennial answers: Next year, Peter said. Two years, Alicia said.

In the end, this exploration of English in a postcommunist state has revealed the loss of a precious moment in time. Every interview presented the same elegy: briefly—after the Velvet Revolution, before the split with the Czech Republic, and before Slovakia's role was articulated in the world economy—it seemed that anything was possible. For so many, English was then about "freedom." It wouldn't remain so. If, as I have been suggesting, languages are litmus tests of the health of the systems in which they participate, the present place of English in people's lives indicates that the current global order has much work to do to live up to its own rhetoric of freedom, equality, and justice.

Let's imagine what the greatest optimists of English as a global language predict: that in short order English will have spread so widely, will be spoken with fluency by so many people, that there will be no more "native" advantage in the English education industry or in business communications. English in this scenario recaptures its old valence as the language of freedom, but it also becomes the key to free trade. Should that hypothetical scenario arise, the Slovak situation to date makes clear that there would still be vast and significant inequities. Even should everyone speak the same English all around the world, or should, just as implausibly, the world cease to care about varieties of English, who the speaker is would nonetheless still matter. English's current relentless marketing, its fragmentation, its position as the language of "dis"communication—all are inextricable from the commercial and political schemes that keep people like Alicia and Peter feeling stuck in motion, bound in freedom.

This feeling, of immobility within movement, was best captured by two comments of Alicia's, one made eleven years after the other. One Saturday afternoon in 1992, Peter, Alicia, and I were looking for a place to eat in the Slovak countryside, only to find the one restaurant for miles around closed. To Alicia, it was idiocy to have a restaurant in an area of the country renowned for recreation closed at the very time people would want to eat. Lacking a great deal of vocabulary in English at that point to communicate her analysis of the situation, she selected one word: "Communism," she said, shaking her head. On an eerily parallel Saturday in 2003, we were ushered out of a restaurant in a mall on the outskirts of Bristol because the mall was closing at seven P.M. Alicia, this time, found it incomprehensible that in a supposedly "capitalist" country—and in what she had been taught was the most capitalist part of the most capitalist country—a restaurant would close at the dinner hour on a weekend night. It reminded her of the absurdity of the rules at her job, but beyond that it reminded her of absurdities she had faced her whole life. As we walked out of the mall toward the car, she declared, "I have been taught all my life that capitalism would become communism, and now I see that it is true."

It seemed from Alicia's comment that capitalism had only succeeded communism by becoming it; no longer under the Cold War mandate to outdo its "other," capitalism could revel in its arbitrary asymmetries. Bureaucracy, cronyism, enforced mediocrity, restrictions placed on routine activities—these were the things Alicia had in mind as she made her comment. Alicia's insight is akin to those views of the world order that have found the failings of communism and the failings of capitalism to be one and the same. Václav Havel has argued that communism and capitalism have both led to social fragmentation and alienation because each economic system is ultimately unconcerned with freedom and dignity. Joseph Stiglitz has observed that communism and capitalism, while often viewed as opposing, share the same failure: both mistakenly idealize a system where power combines with "perfect information" and "perfect virtue."[16]

Stiglitz offers that imagining an economic system without all-pervasive human fallibility is a little like imagining *Othello* without the pernicious Iago. Whereas Havel finds economic systems not human enough, Stiglitz offers that they are inevitably "all too human."

I would add my own addendum to these thoughts, particularly to address idealizations of global English that seem, like idealizations of communism and capitalism, stubborn in their hold on the imagination. Global English is not a technologically perfect medium for the communication of ideas, information, or even friendship. Global English is borders, visas, tabloids, the corporeal bodies that they regulate, and the resources that support them. These, and not various accents or disparities of usage, are the Iago in the play of the lingua franca. The question in the end is not whether English will remain a world language, the knowledge of which will continue to make the wheels of global commerce spin: it may or may not. The critical question is and has always been what kind of world, its good or bad yet to be envisioned, will be shaping it.

Appendix

ENGLISH: A KIND OF SPORT

ME: Your occupation?

PAVOL: Policeman.

ME: Your parents' occupation?

PAVOL: That would be the Russian occupation.

I begin with this 2003 exchange because it sets the scene of the conversations that led to this book. To interview in the wake of an occupation is to interview in an atmosphere of what scholar Danielle Allen would call "congealed distrust."[1] To interview about English, *in* English, leading off with demographic questions often identical to those asked at passport-control stations, is to feel one's words buckle even before they leave one's mouth. When this exchange with Pavol occurred, I actually hadn't even started the interview yet. No tape was rolling, no hard drive spinning. We were in a café where we had agreed to meet to discuss my research; I was telling Pavol the questions in advance so he could decide if he wanted to be interviewed. I described the study: It's about English. It's about English language use and instruction in Slovakia. After I was done explaining the project, he considered it all very carefully and exhaled, blowing smoke. "I don't know," he said with a sideways smile. "This information might be used by the state."

Pavol was clearly enjoying this repartee; he could tell that his pun on "occupation" had scored a hit with me—with one deft expression he had managed to simultaneously show off his English and show up the banality of social science research. Although his sideways smile did not allow me to dismiss his last comment about the misuse of information entirely, it did suggest an element of sport in his approach to English. If English as a lingua franca has been a battlefield—dangerous ground for Slovaks entering a global economy in which they had little hand in making the rules—it has also been exciting ground, a place where new expressions could be created on the fly. Recall that Pavol's encounters with English began during the communist regime as "a kind of sport"—the ability to raise his hand fast enough to beat out his other classmates, all wanting to learn English. Sport is the other side of congealed distrust, an alternative to outright despair. It is equally a mode of defiance to established orders, a way to leave a mark on something—like English—that helps to define one's place in the world.

Not surprisingly, given the climate of uncertainty and distrust that characterizes the postcommunist world, many of the people I interviewed for this book were accessed through social networks. As I described in chapter 4, getting things done in Slovakia was about "who you know." Those who knew me personally, or knew someone who knew me, were most willing to talk to me, though in a way that made sport of distrust. "Why are you asking me this again?" Peter would groan when I pressed for some clarification. "You already know the story, Mossad." "Mossad," the nickname of the Israeli Secret Service, was the diminutive he gave me throughout my research; my transition from friend to researcher was far from smooth. It's true that he, Alicia, Goran, and Jan had been telling me their stories for years, particularly those of oppression during the communist regime, but I hadn't been listening with the kind of ear one uses when a project is in the making and other audiences are imagined. And, of course, there was much pertaining to their particular histories with English I did not know. My aim for every interview, then, whether I had known the interviewee before or not, was the same: to elicit accounts of mundane and exceptional encounters they might have had with English chronologically throughout their lives. For all his irritation with this process, Peter was supportive in his way, ribbing me about all the money I would make from the book. When I explained the actual market in academic publishing, and that in my experience, one didn't make money in that market, Peter paused for a minute and said, "But this book will be interesting, unlike your last book." Often, it seemed, I served as a handy medium through which to say something clever in English.

I met Peter, Alicia, Goran, and Goran's then-wife on the same day in the summer of 1992, through Liza, the British national with whom my colleague Rebecca and I had taught the summer program. Also a freelance English teacher, Liza had been hired by Peter and Alicia the year before. Because Peter actively cultivated relationships with foreigners, and Liza did the same with locals, they quickly became friends. Peter, Goran, and Ruslan (whom I met later) had all known each other since adolescence, when they played on the same volleyball team. It was at technical university that Peter met Alicia. After graduation, Peter and Goran worked in the same biomedical firm; when I met them, they were planning to found a software development company with Alicia. Goran opted to stay at the biomedical firm, rising within its ranks, but Peter and Alicia went on to form the company that would eventually take them and their children to the United Kingdom. Before their emigration, however, Peter and Alicia had become Goran's near neighbors, taking advantage of social networks to move from their apartment in Bratislava to a house a few doors down from Goran and his family, in a village outlying the city.

I met Jan through Peter and Alicia in 1994. My first introduction to him was the car trip I depict at the beginning of chapter 1—the rhapsody on antilock brakes. Although I did not keep systematic field notes in 1994, I did take detailed notes on that first evening with Jan; at the time, it was a way to expunge the vision of the body in the road. In 1994 Jan was dating Goran's then-sister-in-law and employing Goran's then-wife in his law firm. When Peter and Alicia moved to England in 1998, Jan and Goran's sister-in-law (by that time married) rented Peter and Alicia's house in their absence. Jan and Goran became neighbors, their children cousins. In Slovakia, friendship, kinship, and professional networks often overlapped. One of the anxieties evident throughout my research in Slovakia was that globalization would challenge these close ties. As chapter 5 has shown, it did.

The proximity of Goran's house to Jan's played some role in how I wound up interviewing Jan. Always happy for an excuse to drive, Jan had offered to give my husband and me a lift from Goran's house back to Bratislava. On the way he inquired how my interview with Goran had gone and then asked why I hadn't asked him for an interview. I realized that I'd made a strange kind of faux pas. The truth was, I hadn't asked Jan for an interview because he often mentioned being short on time, but my not asking had conveyed the impression that either his English wasn't up to snuff or his story was of no consequence. Already knowing his history of growing up in the UK, I of course had been curious to learn more and was delighted that he was affronted into giving the interview.

The last couple involved in this friendship network is Ruslan and Viola. I met Ruslan, also in Goran's garden, in 1994. He was not yet working for Goran's firm, but he soon would be. Viola had entered this network of friends after joining Goran's firm in the late 1990s and becoming involved with Ruslan. She was considered the "talker" of the group, always with a humorous story to relate. Whatever reservations she may have had about speaking English when she was first hired by Goran, she had clearly overcome them by the time we met. She and Ruslan were married in 2005, with Goran and Peter in attendance (Alicia was stuck in England).

My acquaintance with a second major friendship network in this book is of shorter duration, dating back to meeting Fero and Zlatica in the United States in the spring of 2003. I had been looking for someone to teach me Slovak (no Slovak language course existed on my campus—indeed, only a handful exist in the United States), and colleagues told me about Fero. I emailed him to ask if he knew anyone who might give me Slovak lessons. He responded that yes, he did: his wife, who in Slovakia was a university instructor of Russian and French, would be able to teach me. During that spring and early summer, I spent quite a bit of time at Fero's apartment, working with Zlatica, before they returned to Slovakia that July. When I rejoined them that August at their cabin near Partizánske, I met many of their friends—among them Pavol and Iveta. My husband and I met Pavol subsequently in Bratislava, where he lived and where we were based. Knowing that Pavol traveled to EU and OECD meetings as a representative for Slovakia, I pursued an interview with him, and he, sensing the pursuit, engaged in the sporting repartee noted above. I interviewed Iveta in her flat on one of my visits to Banská Bystrica.

The last time I saw Pavol, Iveta, Fero, and Zlatica was in Fero's sister's apartment in Bratislava, just days before I was due to leave Slovakia. Iveta,

Fero, and Zlatica had come to take the European Union administrator exam the next morning, along with the hundreds of other Slovaks who had applied, among them Jozef. Unlike Jozef, they had only studied on the four-hour car trip from Banská Bystrica to Bratislava. They didn't expect to pass the written portion of the exam, and they didn't. That last evening we spent together, we watched old propaganda programs of communist medal ceremonies on TV. Fero remarked that although he was old enough to remember these programs, his students were not. Communism seemed abstract to them, Fero thought, its oppressions only quaint stories. He further commented that he was beginning to feel old because he knew only one foreign language whereas so many younger Slovaks were achieving fluency in at least two. We talked a little of the lifting of the visa requirement to Britain, which had just been announced. Iveta, who had recently returned from a trip to England during which she had served as a translator for a Slovak group, remarked dryly of the visa's death, "It was long overdue." This phrase took on extra resonance as the communist medal ceremonies droned in the background, recalling the many years of Slovaks' restricted movements.

Outside of these two friendship networks, I spoke with or interviewed at length seven former students, all female. I had sent requests for interviews to all the former students on my class lists whose addresses I could track down, and only females responded. But there were networks at work even here: through the ones I could find, I heard about some of the others. So-and-so was in Australia, so-and-so in Dubai. It was heartwarming to see again one memorable group of friends from the 1994 summer session, still a tight trio in 2003, though only one of the them felt confident enough in her English to be interviewed. She was the au pair who was barred from England for violating the rules on work-term limits. In 2003 she was living in Slovenia with a man she had initially courted in English.

Certainly my relationship with Maria was the most significant of any I had with former students. The guinea pig of the project, she was the first person I interviewed, in Boston, before I made the trip back to Slovakia in 2003. Living not far from us in Bratislava, she and her then-partner Mona were our most constant companions during the term of my research. Through me, Maria and Mona met several people in the other friendship networks. They accompanied Rebecca and Liza (both visiting, both also former teachers of Maria's) and me on a trip to Banská Bystrica, meeting Fero and Zlatica. When Maria and Mona were embroiled in a property dispute with an ex-girlfriend of Mona's, Jan, to whom I described the situation at their urging, offered to arbitrate pro bono. Maria and/or Mona met with Jan several times before the situation was resolved. He eventually drew up the necessary paperwork and served as witness. I was inserted through this situation in an exchange around a question of property and value that had emerged with capitalist integration, though one resolved through the familiar route of social networks.

I would say that conducting the research for this book altered my relationships with many people I had known for years, but the ascendancy of English had already begun that job. When I first arrived in 1992, no one cared that I spoke English, beyond the people I was employed to teach. In 2003, I faced my new capacity as "resource." This change was perhaps most visible in my relationship to Ruza and her family, whom I boarded with in 1992 and 1994 and lived down the street from in 2003. In 1992, Ruza had taken in Rebecca and me for extra money. She had no interest in developing English beyond what she had learned in school and certainly—as a single mother of two young children she was rearing on a small maternity allotment—had little time to herself of any kind. When I returned in 2003, Ruza had taken a position at the National Bank of Slovakia that entailed implementing directives in English from the European Central Bank. Her daughter, a junior in *gymnázium,* was studying English in an attempt to achieve fluency. With a new job and her daughter's maturita examinations looming (her daughter was in the first cohort to take the reformed exam), Ruza was now very interested in improving both her own English and that of her daughter. Every Sunday evening she invited my husband and me over for Slovak food and English conversation, the conversation as substantial as the food. The textbooks and dictionaries were brought out, every question about the daughter's homework presented for answers. What, we were asked to explain, was the difference between *decision* and *determination?* They watched us stumble for words, clearly at sea. Whenever John and I determined (decided?) that either Ruza or her daughter had the correct interpretation of a particularly gnarly grammatical point, a big "ha" ensued from the victorious party. Their playful competition to get things "right," however, exposed cracks in the unitary English they had been given to master—and exposed as well where another competition lay: John and I often walked home bickering over our varying and no doubt regionally inflected interpretations of English usage.

Those whose extensive interviews became the subject of this book were invited to comment on what I wrote about them. Perhaps unsurprisingly (because he knew me best), Peter was the only one to request a change: he was horrified at how his English looked when transcribed exactly and worried that the imperfections of his usage would make him look ignorant or stupid. Given that "Peter" is a pseudonym, and that "Peter" is not likely to be identified, I understood this fear of looking stupid as not being about *him* per se. He didn't want Slovaks to look stupid. Recall Peter's statement that the West regarded Slovaks as if they came "from banana trees." We decided I would paraphrase anything in his own speech that he didn't like. I did not consciously edit anyone else's speech to hew it more closely to any standardized linguistic ideal.

I end on this moment of textual revision because it illustrates the double bind of English that this book is about: Peter saw this book as a way Slovaks could say something "interesting" in English, that interesting thing being that Slovaks were nowhere near as backward as the West imagined; but saying it himself in English, he feared, would only confirm the impression of backwardness, an impression he was weary of confronting. Doubtless a similar weariness on the part of the Slovak government prompted its January 2007 decision to kick the BBC off the Bratislava radio dial. The director of Slovakia's licensing bureau, Ľuboš Kukliš, explained that one of the reasons the BBC's license was not renewed, their frequency reassigned to Radio Lumen, a Catholic radio station broadcasting in Slovak, was that the BBC had begun broadcasting entirely in English, in violation of the Slovak language law that public broadcasts must be in Slovak.[2] This moment of subtle censorship indicates the added ideological weight that English now carries. The resurgence of the language politics of the early 1990s—this time applied to English as well as to minority languages— suggests that the Slovak government is grappling with its marginalized place in an expanding world largely dominated by English.

It is important to note that virtually no one I interviewed would have approved of the government's decision (and neither did the majority of those Slovaks who responded to the news of the BBC cancellation in dis-

cussion forums of the online version of the Slovak language daily *Sme*).[3]
A greater postcommunist weariness would be not with English, but rather
with the imperative to always speak to the collective and the political.
Thus, for me to conclude with the political point that English does not
work equally for all in the global economy seems a betrayal, and indeed a
misrepresentation, of the variety of responses to the global picture emerging from my interviews. Not everyone with whom I spoke shared Peter's
crisis with English. Pavol, for example, was much more confident about his
English than Peter, though he worried that as he continued to teach beginners and communicate with Europeans it would only get worse. Whereas
Peter, living in England, regretted that his English was "only average," Pavol, teaching English in Slovakia, knew that his was above average and
reveled in his status as "king" among the blind. I take Pavol's pun on "occupation," then, as devised as much to show what he, as an individual,
could do with English as to get me to take Slovakia's legacy of occupation
seriously. There were political points to be made through English, but also
artful expression to be crafted; neither one should obscure the other.

To be honest, it pained me to accede to Peter's request for editing. In
my own foolish way, I had looked forward to capturing in this book the so-
often-missed Peter and Alicia in the language in which I best knew them,
which was their English, not mine. I saw in their Englishes—indeed in
the English of everyone I interviewed—a revivification of a language that
had seemed to me dead when I spoke it. I did not see these Englishes as a
way to understand "their" culture; rather, I wanted to write in these Englishes in order to collapse the distances—political, economic, and geographic—that had, as Maria put it so well but so tentatively, "estranged"
all of us. I understand the tangled metaphors and constructions that often
result from failure to reproduce perfectly another's language as the best
hope for maintaining the vitality and spirit of communication, the best
hope for expanding the sense of what can be expressed, what meanings
can be made. With this thought I leave this book on the note of naive hope
on which it began.

Notes

INTRODUCTION

1. See Nickerson, "English as a *Lingua Franca*," for a review of research on English as a lingua franca in multinational business.

2. The preference of American social scientists for the term *postsocialist* over the term *postcommunist* notwithstanding, I use *postcommunist* because my interlocutors overwhelmingly referred to the socio-politico-economic construct of the era post–World War II and pre-1989 as "communism."

3. Wood, "Europe's Great Divide"; Reynolds, "Once a Backwater"; "Transformed."

4. These reforms included introducing flexibility in labor laws so that employers could more easily fire workers. See World Bank, *Doing Business in 2005*.

5. See Watkins, *Everyday Exchanges,* for a discussion of the "common sense" of capitalism.

6. Prices are listed in Akadémia Vzdelávania of Bratislava's price sheet for the 2003–4 school year. Akadémia Vzdelávania is an established not-for-profit academy.

7. "Na bezchybnú angličtinu treba operáciu jazyka"; message board posting, Jan. 7, 2004.

8. Rogers, "National Agendas and the Communication Divide," 84; Caldwell, "Unavoidable English Language," 7.

9. Phillipson, *English-Only Europe?* 145.

10. Crystal, *English as a Global Language,* 83.

11. Joseph E. Stiglitz and Bruce Greenwald explain: "Every piece of information produced must be different from any other piece of information produced (otherwise it is not new knowledge)" (*Towards a New Paradigm in Monetary Economics,* 149).

12. Stephen Levitt and Steven Dubner discuss the information asymmetries involved in these scandals in *Freakonomics.*

13. Stergios Leventis and Pauline Weetman found that companies reporting in two languages instead of one are responding to market pressures and that these companies typically disclose more; see "Impression Management." For a discussion of the "noise" created by companies, see Stiglitz, *Whither Socialism?* 41.

14. This surge, of course, was established through reforms of the labor and welfare structure. These reforms were viewed by the World Bank as in line with the 2002 EU Council meeting in Lisbon, which was set up "to make the EU the most competitive and dynamic knowledge-based economy in the world." See World Bank, *Quest for Equitable Growth,* 2.

15. See Nancy M. Henley and Cheris Kramarae's discussion of how communication hierarchies between men and women allow men to be less adept at interpreting women's utterances: "Gender, Power, and Miscommunication."

16. Berdahl, Bunzl, and Lampland, *Altered States.*

17. A 1986 British Council report on the state of English teaching in Czechoslovakia gives some indication of the potential opportunities for Czechoslovak citizens to hear spoken English from British or American nationals. Three British Council–recruited lecturers were employed at three different universities in Slovakia, mostly for teacher training. Further, nineteen British Council lecturers taught in a summer program for teachers of English. Opportunities for English teachers to converse with English or American first-language English speakers were rare, then, beyond their training. The report notes that Czechoslovakia was, of socialist countries, particularly insulated from spoken English language programs: "Czechoslovakia is one of the few socialist countries not to take BBC radio or television ELT [English language teaching] programmes. There are radio programmes for schools' English but they are not widely enough used to be significant. An exception is in Bratislava where for the past four years the British Council–recruited lecturer has presented programmes which have attracted quite a following" (4). As a result, the study notes, reading was the most developed English language skill, with very little improvement in practical language use. See British Council, "English Teaching Profile."

Jan Průcha, a Czech linguist, also found reading in the 1980s to be the more developed English language skill. He further determined that English was less used than German and Russian (although he reached this conclusion drawing on data from a 1965 study on uses of foreign languages by Czechoslovak citizens). He determined the distribution of foreign language use to be (1) German (43.6 percent of all communicative acts), (2) Russian (29.1 percent), and (3) English (14.5 percent). Průcha adds, however: "There were significant differences between the particular foreign languages concerning the use for various communicative purposes, topics of communication and regularity of communication. For example, the most frequent communicative activities were: In German—ordinary social conversation; in Russian—oral communication for specific working purposes; in

English—reading and translating texts for specific working purposes" ("Foreign Language Needs," 109, ERIC 6). Průcha estimates that the same patterns of use obtained in 1984, with some increase in English and some decrease in German.

18. European Commission, *Key Data on Education,* 74.

19. For a discussion of "macroaquisition," see Brutt-Griffler, *World English.* Brutt-Griffler distinguishes two types of language spread: one that occurs when speakers of a language migrate and one ("macroaquisition") that occurs when a community or group takes up the task of acquiring a language.

20. With the influence of global pop and particularly hip-hop culture now pervasive in Bratislava, in 2008 this student would not have stood out.

21. Larson, "Selling Oneself."

22. See Castle, "Brussels Receives 21,000 CV's." Castle records that the salaries advertised for one thousand temporary EU administrator positions ranged from over 25,000 euro to over 184,000 euro per month.

23. Interestingly, I have run across the phrase "the so-called Velvet Revolution" in the literature on education reform. See Švec, "Reforming General Education," 73. Unlike Jozef, however, Švec clearly is being unironic. He believes much in the area of educational policy has changed.

24. As Stiglitz explains, part of the reason a supply-and-demand economy works to the extent that it does is because people believe in it. See Stiglitz, "Information and the Change in the Paradigm."

25. The United Nations Development Programme's *Human Development Report 1999,* with its overview entitled "Globalization with a Human Face," asks that the interdependence produced by globalization work for individuals, not merely for the bottom line. On July 30–31, 2003, UNESCO and the UN hosted an international conference in Tokyo: "Globalization with a Human Face—Benefitting All." Stiglitz ends his *Globalization and Its Discontents* with a call for globalization with "a human face." Finally, Mark Rupert notes that the phrase, used by Bill Clinton and the World Bank, serves as a site of struggle and contestation as it is evoked to mean different things in different contexts. See Rupert, *Ideologies of Globalization.*

26. Michael Ferrary determines that bankers often engage in creating social networks (through informal activities like golfing with clients, etc.) not to build friendly relationships but to gain more information about potential risks. See "Trust and Social Capital."

27. For perspectives on British and/or American colonialism and English, see Phillipson's *Linguistic Imperialism;* Pennycook's *English and the Discourses of Colonialism;* and Canagarajah's pointed response to Phillipson, *Resisting Linguistic Imperialism.*

28. All efforts were made to occlude the identity of the participants, except for one who chose to be identifiable.

CHAPTER 1

1. His fluency in English, for example, far exceeded that of the director of the English language summer program that employed me.

2. Excellent discussions of "normalization" can be found in Innes, *Czechoslovakia;* and Leff, *Czech and Slovak Republics.*

3. See Eyal, *Origins of Postcommunist Elites.*

4. Havel, *Open Letters,* 344–45.

5. The 1986 British Council report asserts that study of English had "overtaken" German in popularity, but that many more students were being thwarted in their efforts to study English in school by the dictates of the controlled labor market: "English is the most popular option being studied by some 87,000 pupils. More would do so if the authorities did not need to keep the teachers of French and German occupied." The report also notes that no new teachers of English had been admitted to university for training because few teachers on the market had retired: "Intake into some English departments was reduced between 1982 and 1985 because of a decline in the number of teaching posts available" ("English Teaching Profile," 3). In short, English teachers were not being hired widely. Mary Schleppengrell notes that they were also not being trained in the 1980s: "In Brno, Czechoslovakia, for example, the Pedagogical Faculty had not graduated any English teachers since 1977, but began a training program in September 1990, with 45 students of English" ("Teaching English in Central Europe," 7). Jan Průcha notes that students nevertheless tended to choose English over German where they could, even though they had fewer opportunities to use the language. He observes that a shift in language preferences was taking place in the country, as older adults tended to value German more, but their children, often influenced by pop music, tended to be more interested in English. He suggests that even more students would choose to study English, if given a choice ("Foreign Language Needs"). Another source revealing of the actual state of student choice in their curriculum is Stanislav Vodinský's *Schools in Czechoslovakia.* In a defense of the centralized control of educational options, Vodinský bemoans student interest in the humanities as "out of proportion" with the needs of the state: "The boys' and girls' interest in the humanities is still quite out of proportion; this becomes apparent already at the level of the general secondary in the selection of streams. Places in the mathematical-physics stream are filled with greater difficulty" (34). The undesirable result, he notes, is that there were still not enough applicants for the number of technical universities that had been built.

6. That the purpose of education under the communist regime in Czechoslovakia was to create individuals who would be useful in fulfilling the needs of the state is succinctly stated by Vodinský: "The school becomes closely linked to the urgent demands of life, to the building of socialism in the country" (*Schools in Czechoslovakia,* 7).

7. The 1986 British Council report notes, "Almost the only British books on

sale are a very poor selection of scientific and technical works at about four times their UK price." Universities, the report continues, "have pathetically inadequate funds for Western books. A leading university English department, for example, was allowed to buy only six titles a year" ("English Teaching Profile," 2). Although the British Council was able to make some presentations of books, American presentations of books were prohibited. On the subject of English language instruction in secondary schools, the British Council report records a paucity of materials aside from the centrally prescribed "stodgy" textbook. Nevertheless, English was studied in schools, particularly at the secondary level, but the extent of study is difficult to reconstruct in Slovakia during the period of normalization. Studies have been conducted on both sides of the Iron Curtain, but their accounts emerge from different sources and methods of data collection. Further complicating matters is the fact that Slovakia was at that point part of Czechoslovakia, and few accounts treat the Slovak region specifically. The *Pedagogická encyklopédia Slovenska* is notable in this regard, recording that in 1980, 2.84 percent of students at normal primary schools (4,943 of 173,913) chose English as an elective (it was not widely offered outside of special schools at the primary level). The report offers that 40.61 percent of students from general secondary schools (21,576 of 53,134) were learning English. See *Pedagogická encyklopédia Slovenska.* Mary Schleppengrell estimates that as of November 1989, only 16 percent of Czechoslovaks had the opportunity to study a foreign language other than Russian, but this estimate is almost certainly too low, given that students attending *gymnáziá* were required to study a foreign language in addition to Russian. (For a discussion of secondary school requirements, see Státní Pedagogické Nakladatelství, *Tridsat' rokov socialistického školstva,* vol. 2.) Průcha's estimate that 32 percent of "young people" in Czechoslovakia in the 1980s were learning "obligatorily at least two foreign languages" (including Russian) is probably more accurate ("Foreign Language Needs," 106–7). The Slovak Office of Statistics does not keep a record of how many students chose to study English during this period.

8. Gayatri Spivak acknowledges the limits of Marxism as a blueprint for activism: "There is no state on the globe today that is not part of the capitalist economic system or can want to eschew it fully. In fact, within the economic sphere, Marxism—at its best as a speculative morphology devised by an activist-philosopher who had taught himself contemporary economics enough to see it as a human (because social) science, and through this perception launched a thoroughgoing critique of political economy—can operate in today's world only as a persistent critique of a system—micro-electronic post-industrial world capitalism—that a polity cannot not want to inhabit, for that is the 'real' of the situation" (*Critique of Postcolonial Reason,* 84).

9. For discussions of the many unofficial economies supported by social networks during communism, see Berdahl, *Where the World Ended;* Verdery, *What Was Socialism?*

10. After 1989, when the state language school's monopoly had collapsed and the credential it offered was superseded by external credentials such as TOEFL and the Cambridge certificates, the school was distinguished by being the only language school with declining numbers of students. See Togneri, "English—No Longer a Hobby," 4.

11. Other Slovak women living in millennial England shared Alicia's complaints about British parenting. Zuzana Búriková's ethnographic research on Slovak au pairs working in London documents that they generally found British children spoiled and British mothers uncaring and domestically inept. See "Prečo majú britské matky au pair."

12. Havel, *Open Letters*, 346.

13. The proverb in Slovak is "Koľko jazykov vieš, toľkokrát si človekom." The EU report translates the expression as follows: "The more languages you know, the more of a person you are." See Commission of the European Communities, *Communication*, 1. Peter felt the English word *human* best captured the sense of the proverb.

14. As Susan Gal has observed, the European Union is not genuinely celebratory of the human elements of language; it finds linguistic diversity more troubling than enriching: "Among the political elites of the European Union, the plurality of languages is considered, at best, a matter of ethnolinguistic pride and touristic interest. It merely burdens the bureaucracy with an expensive army of translators, the need for elite multilingualism and for careful diplomacy about language use" ("Contradictions of Standard Language," 163).

15. To this day he will not tell me the camp's actual location.

16. In the nearly three decades between 1936–37 and 1963–64, the number of students who attended vocational training centers and related schools (*stredné odborné učilištia*) in Czechoslovakia doubled, increasing from 168,409 to 326,597. For these students, a school-leaving exam was merely optional, and chances of continuing on to any form of higher education were minimal. The number of pupils in secondary technical schools (*stredné odborné školy*) in that same period in Czechoslovakia increased from 75,522 to 176,591. Also during the same period, the number of pupils attending *gymnázia* in Czechoslovakia decreased from 144,404 to 88,155 (Vodinský, *Schools in Czechoslovakia*, 123–24). By 1980 in Czechoslovakia, 49 percent of youth at age fifteen attended vocational training centers, 23 percent attended technical secondary schools, and another 15 percent attended *gymnázia* (Krian,*World Education Encyclopedia*, 293).

17. The move toward technical education did, as Zlatica suggested, disproportionately affect men. In 1950, females constitued 36.5 percent of *gymnázia* students, 45 percent of students in technical secondary schools, and 20 percent of students in vocational training centers. In 1960, the percentage of female students in *gymnáziá* had increased to nearly 62 percent, in technical secondary training schools to 58 percent, whereas the percentage of vocational training

center students who were women was less than 35 percent (Krian, *World Education Encyclopedia*, 294).

18. *Schools in Czechoslovakia* explains that student assignment to secondary schools was not based on grades or performance on tests alone, but was rather determined by "a special commission," including (at that time, at least) "the headmaster of the school as chairman and members of the local national committee, mass organisations, departments of labour, and representatives of the Association of Parents and Friends of the School" (Vodinský, *Schools in Czechoslovakia*, 58). The commission would produce a report including a detailed description of each student's character, talent, diligence, and interests. Pupils could protest the decision, but the burden of proof was on them. Krian's 1981 report describes the quota system that governed higher education admissions, documenting that some programs, like art schools, were the most popular, with up to five applicants for each place. He records that "curriculum reforms and academic advisory services in secondary schools" attempted to direct more students into technical fields of study (*World Education Encyclopedia*, 303).

19. The significance of this philosophy to the promotion of technical education is outlined in the 1958 state-produced volume *Education in Czechoslovakia*. Written in English and therefore explicitly intended for a Western audience, the volume's foreword bluntly outlines how the emphasis on technical, practical education fulfilled the pedagogical principles of the socialist ideal: "In the past too much emphasis was laid on one-sided theoretical instruction, dialectic mutual relations between theory and practice being ignored and the importance of practice for theoretical knowledge overlooked. Polytechnical education, the importance of which was underlined by pioneers of socialism, has become an indispensable component of the education of young people" (Chlup, Foreword 8). See also Popkewitz, *Paradigm and Ideology*, for an extended discussion of Marxist-Leninist pedagogy.

20. Hardt and Negri, *Empire*, 179.

21. Although Czechoslovakia did not experience anything near the political liberalization of neighboring Poland and Hungary in the late 1980s, Adrian Smith does document "limited attempts at economic reforms," instituted in 1988 to counter widespread discontent over the economy. See *Reconstructing the Regional Economy*, 98. Carol Skalnik Leff notes that by 1988, the government had ceased to jam broadcasts of Radio Free Europe and other broadcasts from the West, leading to "an increasingly information rich environment." See *Czech and Slovak Republics*, 76.

CHAPTER 2

1. Katherine Verdery compares the various factions promoting ethnonationalism in postcommunist states in *What Was Socialism?* Ethnonationalism in the former Soviet bloc was read by the Western world (too simplistically, Verdery

convincingly argues) as the revival of ancient grudges that had been kept at bay by Soviet imperialism rather than as a response to specifically postcommunist transitions, with their accompanying anxieties over who would now be in charge.

2. For a cogent history of this legislation and subsequent legislation governing the use of minority languages, see Gramma, "Working Papers 23." Szabolcs Simon and Miklós Kontra note that the 1990 Law No. 428 on the Official Language of the Slovak Republic was taken as an affirmative rationale for changing Hungarian road signs and the spelling of Hungarian last names, even though the law itself did not specify such changes ("Slovak Linguists and Slovak Language Laws").

3. See Abby Innes, *Czechoslovakia: The Short Goodbye* (New Haven: Yale University Press, 2001). The enforcement of Slovak in traditionally Hungarian dominated towns was seen in part as payback for the forced Magyarization of Slovaks during the Austro-Hungarian Empire's reign in the region. As Ladislav Holý documents, Hungarians were never imagined as a constituency of the new Slovak state. Cries of "Hungarians across the Danube!" had accompanied cries of "We've had enough of Prague" during a nationalistic demonstration in Bratislava in 1990 (*The Little Czech*, 109). I would add here that the Roma, Slovakia's other large linguistic minority, were also disenfranchised by the 1995 language law but were more generally disenfranchised in all spheres.

4. My observation here that English was not the target of these laws is limited to the immediate postcommunist, pre-EU period in Slovakia.

5. In making this point, I am inspired by A. Suresh Canagarajah, who argues that merely noting that powers such as Britain had a vested interest in spreading their language abroad does not in and of itself explain the local interest of people in the periphery in learning that language (*Resisting Linguistic Imperialism in English Teaching*).

6. Most people I interviewed stated a preference for the American accent. They said they felt American accents sounded more pleasant than British accents. As I discuss in chapter 5, however, this preference might also have reflected the deteriorating relations between Slovakia and the UK.

7. For a description of this turn toward the free market, see Mesežnikov, Kollár, and Nicholson, *Slovakia 2002.*

8. For more on these demonstrations, see Innes, *Czechoslovakia*, 258.

9. See Daučíková, Bútorová, and Wallace-Lorencová, "Status of Sexual Minorities." Although gay and lesbian organizations were formed in Slovakia beginning in 1989, adopting international language and organizing tactics to survive, their membership was mainly anonymous, and given widespread heteronormative attitudes, the gay community was largely invisible. It was certainly invisible to Maria, who did not remember having met anyone who was a lesbian until 1997.

10. Rhetorician and art critic Kenneth Burke is eloquent on the subject of art as an act of translation: "The artist begins with his emotion, he translates this emotion into a mechanism for arousing emotion in others, and thus his interest in his own emotion transcends into his interest in the treatment" (*Counter-Statement,* 55).

11. I never heard Fero make a negative comment about the Roma, Hungarians, or Jews, even though such comments, particularly about the Roma in 2003, were common and widely, if not completely, acceptable.

12. Marx, *Capital* I, 80.

13. In the early 1990s, book-length catalogs of agricultural and leisure-related jobs in Great Britain were available in Slovak, and agencies emerged to place temporary workers abroad.

14. Henderson, *Slovakia.*

CHAPTER 3

1. Kollmannová, Bubeníková, and Kopecká, *Angličtina pre samoukov,* 15.

2. Kollmannová, *Angličtina pre samoukov,* 15.

3. Kollmannová, *Angličtina pre samoukov,* 156.

4. Val Rust comments on the change in textbooks in several postcommunist states: "All curricula, textbooks, and instruction related to the inculcation of communist values have been abolished" ("Education Responses to Reforms," 387).

5. Rainer Ganahl notes that possessing a language is unlike exchanging a commodity: the former demands a great deal of time. Unlike finite objects (loaves of bread and quarts of milk), languages are social phenomena and, as a result, are continually changing. Complete knowledge of a language cannot be individually acquired instantly through the exchange of any sum of money. While one cannot own a language, Ganahl suggests that the ability to patent and copyright words amounts to ownership of parts of language, or rather "language games," pace Wittgenstein. See Ganahl, "Free Markets." The English language teaching industry in Slovakia is a type of language game in that it represents the commodification of English, a continual, unending process.

6. See *Development of Education 1990–1992.* This report discusses the novelty of adult education and the importance of language training in that education.

7. Gregory Andrusz writes of job insecurity in the postcommunist world: "The individual has to spend considerable effort engaged in self-promotional strategies. Lacking *social* security, they have to enter into contracts to buy accommodation and health insurance and take out private pensions and pay, when necessary, for further education or training in order to improve their 'marketability'" ("From Wall to Mall," 31).

8. Fico's comments are documented in "Česi a Slováci spomínali na

November." Fico was elected prime minister in 2006. Shortly thereafter, he was castigated by European socialists for forming a coalition that included Mečiar's People's Party—Movement for a Democratic Slovakia.

9. Viola's work with rodents was only a partial fulfillment of her true desire—to study sharks. A citizen of a landlocked country, Viola was stuck with mice. Perhaps this unsatisfactory circumstance also contributed to her overall disappointment with her work.

10. See Bútorová, Filadelfiová, Gyárfášová, Cviková, and Farkašová, "Women, Men, and Equality of Opportunities."

11. For a more detailed discussion of the 1990s inflation in housing prices and consumer goods, see Stolarnik, "Political, Economic, and Cultural Situation."

12. Iveta did not like all the recent changes that globalization—in particular European Union accession—had brought. She was, at the time we spoke, in October 2003, annoyed that the BBC World Service had just been dropped from her region's cable television package and replaced by Euronews, a channel broadcasting primarily in English, but decidedly not "BBC English." (Its online edition, e.g., deferred toward American spellings of words like *favorite*.) Unlike Fero, who bought a satellite so he could access BBC on both radio and TV, Iveta, ever adaptable, resigned herself to the new state of affairs: "I still haven't got used to Euronews. For me it is something completely different. But we'll watch Euronews if this is the only channel in English." Euronews, with its head office based in France, also broadcasted in French, German, and Spanish.

13. In 2003, unemployment, although negligible in the Bratislava area, rose to almost 40 percent in parts of Eastern Slovakia where the economy had been dominated by the now-defunct Soviet arms industry. Accurate figures that include unemployment of Romany people are difficult to obtain.

14. Slovakia in 2003 was in the midst of fulfilling an EU mandate to consolidate all antidiscrimination legislation into a coherent law, but it had yet to do so. Job advertisements in Slovakia sometimes stated that they would only consider applicants up to a certain age.

15. Kucharíková, Slavin, and Galata, *English for Students of Mechanical Engineering*, 21.

16. The British Council, England's embodiment of the English language teaching industry, had its own motives for being in Slovakia. Robert Phillipson cites British Council documents that show that the organization thought of the English language as England's "black gold" and was concerned with exploiting it to the hilt, maintaining dominance in the English language teaching industry (*English-Only Europe?* 150).

17. Present during my conversation with Fero about Senator Joseph McCarthy (see chapter 1), Pavol chimed in that McCarthy was an American hero, that without the efforts of men like him, communism would have spread to the United States too. He further felt that the American president in 2003, George W.

Bush, was a good leader because he pursued America's interests around the world. Someone in the world, he reasoned, had to be the policeman.

18. Pavol estimated about 70 percent of his work took place in English.

19. Zábojová, Peprník, and Nangonová, *Angličtina I. pre samoukov a kurzy,* 211.

20. Pension amounts and retirement ages for Slovakia in 2001 can be found in Radičová, "Social Policy," 549.

21. Kollmannová, *Angličtina pre samoukov,* 438.

CHAPTER 4

1. For reasons of preserving anonymity, I have not identified the exact office of the Ministry of Education charged with developing and executing the reform. Throughout the chapter, I refer to this office as "the Ministry," although the relationship of this office to the minister of education, as this chapter suggests, was hardly seamless. In the public perception, there was really little distinction between this particular office and the actual Ministry of Education. Failures in the execution of the exam (discussed in this chapter) nonetheless laid directly at the door of the minister of education.

2. Strictly speaking, there was no official designation "reform team." This moniker was used often by members of the group, however, perhaps to invoke more official regard than the entity assembled actually had.

3. Mary Schleppengrell records the general unease regarding the use of requalified Russian teachers and uncertified native speakers to meet the postcommunist demand for English language teachers: "Parents are pressuring schools to provide English instruction beginning at the primary level, and for many principals it is tempting to respond by hiring either Russian teachers with rudimentary English skills or native speakers with no background in pedagogy or methods. Language teaching professionals in these countries fear that these practices will lower the standard for English teaching" ("Teaching English in Central Europe," 12). One of the maturita reform team members I spoke with ranked international organizations by English teacher quality. Some international organizations, she suggested, could be relied on to train English speakers to be teachers, while others could not.

4. See Ministry of Education, "Hodnota maturitnej skúšky dnes a zajtra."

5. For a discussion of the 2005 controversy, see Jurinová, "Trouble over Tests." Also see Petková, "Vyzradila sa aj maturitaz angličtiny," which documents the problems with the 2006 tests.

6. Deborah Brandt makes the benefits that accrue to sponsors of literacy initiatives clear: "Sponsors are delivery systems for the economies of literacy, the means by which these forces present themselves to—and through—individual learners. They also represent the causes into which people's literacy usually gets recruited. . . . Usually richer, more knowledgeable, and more entrenched than the sponsored, sponsors nevertheless enter a reciprocal relationship with those

they underwrite. They lend their resources or credibility to the sponsored but also stand to gain benefits from their success, whether by direct repayment or, indirectly, by credit of association" (*Literacy in American Lives,* 19).

7. Through this same period, stories about bribery in the health care system, another state-supported sector of the economy, were almost daily features in the newspapers.

8. Announcement posted on the British Council of Slovakia's Web site: http://www.britishcouncil.org/slovakia-education-projects.htm (accessed Apr. 21, 2006).

9. Phillips, "British Council a reforma maturity na Slovensku."

10. Bérešová, Hosszúová, and Macková, *Nová maturita z angličtiny,* 187.

11. Bérešová, Hosszúová, and Macková, *Nová maturita z angličtiny,* 187.

12. Jaroslava did not mention whether these museum items were dated to the period when Slovakia was part of the Kingdom of Hungary.

13. Bérešová, Hosszúová, and Macková, *Nová maturita z angličtiny,* 236.

14. This visit was the only part of the meeting that took place in Slovak. The visiting representative from the Ministry didn't know English.

15. Akadémia vzdelávania offered a maturita preparation course in spring of 2007 at a rate of 7,000 Slovak crowns for fifty hours of instruction. See http://www.aveducation.sk/ (accessed Mar. 15, 2007).

16. See http://www.britishcouncil.org/slovakia-english-our-courses.htm#maturita (accessed Mar. 13, 2007).

17. This suddenly blunt assessment of the drafted materials might also have been enabled by the absence of Jaroslava, who had left the afternoon before.

CHAPTER 5

1. Drakulič, *Café Europa,* 14.

2. Pennycook, "Beyond Homogeny and Heterogeny," 6.

3. Robert Phillipson famously charged David Crystal's *English as a Global Language* with presenting a "triumphalist" account of the rise of English. See "Voice in Global English."

4. Stiglitz, *Globalization and Its Discontents,* 213.

5. Tony Judt observes that the French were horrified by the realization that French was no longer the language of Europe but perhaps even more horrified that the default language of communication in Brussels, as in the rest of the world, had become English. Eastern Europeans, particularly the young, Judt notes, were quick to perceive that to be "European" meant to speak English (*Postwar,* 759).

6. Peter, recall from chapter 1, had been barred from medical school by the communist regime. He had nevertheless found a way to use his technical training in the health field.

7. A critical disagreement over steel production between Slovakia and the EU

erupted during my fieldwork. The EU argued that U.S. Steel Košice, the entity that had emerged after U.S. Steel bought Slovakia's formerly state-run steel enterprise, had failed to adhere to EU production quotas. France and Germany had exceeded their national debt limit during the same period and were forgiven, while Slovakia, in order to join the EU, was forced to adhere to the limit.

8. Fila, "Making Fun of the Roma."

9. The database was provided by an outside contractor, whose name representatives at Orange declined to reveal, citing contractual considerations.

10. All these comments on the article "Making Fun of the Roma" can be found at http://www.slovakspectator.sk (accessed Apr. 3, 2006).

11. Indeed, the international circulation of the Roma jokes, the story about the jokes, and the commentary about the story is an example of the modern circulation of texts, genres, and ideologies that, as Susan Gal observes, constitutes the European public sphere in the absence of an official, institutionally functional public sphere. As Gal rightly points out, public spheres do not in and of themselves ensure democracy, even where a common language is used ("Contradictions of Standard Language").

12. Denis MacShane's comments are documented in "Those Roamin' Roma."

13. "Those Roamin' Roma."

14. The image of Slovakia as a poor, uncivilized country has been conveyed not only through written English but also through the Hollywood industry. Two major recent films, *Eurotrip* (2004) and *Hostel* (2006), represent Slovakia as a deprived and depraved country. In *Eurotrip,* Slovaks pour sewage out of the windows of their flats, and old men bathe themselves in the streets. In the popular blockbuster *Hostel,* Slovak women trap and sell backpackers to Westerners craving the experience of killing other humans, and roving bands of starving Slovak children threaten to kill tourists for candy. In a feature about the making of the film, *Hostel* director Eli Roth jokes with Slovak actress Barbara Nedeljaková that Slovaks eat parrots. Barbara Nedeljaková (identified in the segment as "Slovakia Apologist") tries to counter the representation of Slovakia in the film: "We don't have children who try to kill you for chewing gum. I never saw that. It's a beautiful country, with normal people. Nice."

15. One Slovak au pair for a British family reported that she could clean the whole house in the time it took the mother to chop a carrot. See Búriková, "Prečo majú britské matky au pair."

16. Stiglitz, "Public Policy for a Knowledge Economy."

APPENDIX

1. Allen, *Talking to Strangers,* xiii.

2. See, e.g., "BBC si na Slovensku nenaladíme."

3. Some of the commentators in the discussion forum noted that Radio Lumen already had a spot on the dial.

Bibliography

Allen, Danielle. *Talking to Strangers.* Chicago: University of Chicago Press, 2004.

Andrusz, Gregory. "From Wall to Mall." In *Winds of Societal Change: Remaking Post-Communist Cities,* ed. Zorica Nedovic-Budic and Sasha Tsenkova, 21–42. Champaign: Russian, East European, and Eurasian Center at University of Illinois at Urbana-Champaign, 2004.

"BBC si na Slovensku nenaladíme." *Sme,* January 31, 2007. http://www.sme.sk/c/3122053/BBC-si-na-Slovensku-nenaladime.html (accessed January 31, 2007).

Berdahl, Daphne. *Where the World Ended: Re-Unification and Identity in the German Borderland.* Berkeley: University of California Press, 1999.

Berdahl, Daphne, Matti Bunzl, and Martha Lampland, eds. *Altered States: Ethnographies of Transition in Eastern Europe and the Former Soviet Union.* Ann Arbor: University of Michigan Press, 2000.

Bérešová, Jana, Marta Hosszúová, and Marta Macková. *Nová maturita z angličtiny: príprava na maturitu y anglického jazyka.* Bratislava: Aktuell, 2000.

Brandt, Deborah. *Literacy in American Lives.* New York: Cambridge University Press, 2001.

British Council. "English Teaching Profile: Czechoslovakia." London: British Council, February 1986. ERIC Document Reproduction Service No. ED 268 779.

Brutt-Griffler, Janina. *World English: A Study of Its Development.* Clevedon: Multilingual Matters, 2002.

Búriková, Zuzana. "Prečo Majú Britské Matky Au Pair a Čo sa na Tom Slovenským Au Pair Nepáči." *Slovenský Národopis* 54, no. 3 (2006): 341–56.

Burke, Kenneth. *Counter-Statement.* Berkeley: University of California Press, 1968.

Bútorová, Zora, Jarmila Filadelfiová, Ol'ga Gyárfášová, Jana Cviková, and Katarína Farkašová. "Women, Men, and Equality of Opportunities." In Mesežnikov, Kollár, and Nicholson, *Slovakia 2002,* 719–42.

Caldwell, Christopher. "The Unavoidable English Language." *Financial Times* (U.S. ed.), September 24, 2005, 7.

Canagarajah, A. Suresh. *Resisting Linguistic Imperialism in English Teaching.* New York: Oxford University Press, 1999.

Castle, Stephen. "Brussels Receives 21,000 CV's from Eastern Europe in Recruiting Drive." *Independent,* February 20, 2003. http://findarticles.com/p/articles/mi_qn4158/is_20030220/ai_n12678693 (accessed July 31, 2007).

"Česi a Slováci spomínali na november." *Sme Online,* November 18, 2003. http://www.sme.sk/c/1170496/Cesi-a-Slovaci-spominali-na-november.html.

Chlup, Otokar. Foreword. In *Education in Czechoslovakia,* ed. Státní pedagogické Nakladatelství, 7–9. Prague: Státní pedagogické nakladatelství, 1958.

Commission of the European Communities. *Communication from the Commission to the Council, the European Parliament, the European Economic and Social Committee and the Committee of the Regions: A New Framework Strategy for Multilingualism.* Brussels. November 22, 2005.

Crystal, David. *English as a Global Language.* Cambridge: Cambridge University Press, 2003.

Daučíková, Anna, Zora Bútorová, and Viera Wallace-Lorencová. "The Status of Sexual Minorities." In Mesežnikov, Kollár, and Nicholson, *Slovakia 2002,* 743–56.

Development of Education 1990–1992: Czech and Slovak Federal Republic. International Conference on Education, 43rd session, Geneva, 1992. Bratislava: Institute of Information and Prognoses of Education, Youth, and Sports, 1992.

Drakulič, Slavenka. *Café Europa: Life after Communism.* New York: Penguin, 1996.

European Commission. *Key Data on Education in the European Union—1997.* Luxemburg: Office for Official Publications of the European Communities, 1997.

Eyal, Gil. *The Origins of Postcommunist Elites: From the Prague Spring to the Breakup of Czechoslovakia.* Minneapolis: University of Minnesota Press, 2003.

Ferrary, Michael. "Trust and Social Capital in the Regulation of Lending Activities." *Journal of Socio-Economics* 31, no. 6 (2003): 673–99.

Fila, Lukaš. "Making Fun of the Roma." *Slovak Spectator,* September 8, 2003. http://www.slovakspectator.sk/clanok.asp?vyd=2003034&cl=13774 (accessed April 3, 2006).

Gal, Susan. "Contradictions of Standard Language in Europe: Implications for the Study of Practices and Publics." *Social Anthropology* 14, no. 2 (2006): 163–81.

Ganahl, Rainer. "Free Markets: Language, Commodification, and Art." *Public Culture* 13, no.1 (2001): 24–25.

Gottheinerová, Till, and Sergej Tryml. *A Handbook of English Conversation.* Prague: Státní pedagogické nakladatelstvi, 1970.

Gramma, Gizella Szabómihály. "Working Papers 23: Language Policy and Language Rights in Slovakia." Barcelona: Escarré International Centre for Ethnic Minorities and Nations, 2006.

Hardt, Michael, and Antonio Negri. *Empire.* Cambridge: Harvard University Press, 2000.

Havel, Václav. *Open Letters: Selected Writings, 1965–1990.* Ed. Paul Wilson. New York: Knopf, 1991.

Henderson, Karen. *Slovakia: The Escape from Invisibility.* New York: Routledge, 2002.

Henley, Nancy M., and Cheris Kramarae. "Gender, Power, and Miscommunication." In *"Miscommunication" and Problematic Talk,* ed. Nikolas Coupland, Howard Giles, and John Wiemann, 18–43. Newbury Park: Sage, 1991.

Holý, Ladislav. *The Little Czech and the Great Czech Nation: National Identity and the Post-Communist Social Transformation.* New York: Cambridge University Press, 1996.

Innes, Abby. *Czechoslovakia: The Short Goodbye.* New Haven: Yale University Press, 2001.

Judt, Tony. *Postwar.* New York: Penguin, 2005.

Jurinová, Martina. "Trouble over Tests." *Slovak Spectator,* April 25, 2005. http://www.slovakspectator.sk/default-2005016.html (accessed May 30, 2006).

Kollmannová, Ludmila. *Angličtina pre samoukov.* Slovak ed. Bratislava: Vydavatel'stvo Smaragd Pedagogické Nakladatel'stvo, 1997.

Kollmannová, Ludmila, Libuše Bubeníková, and Alena Kopecká. *Angličtina pre samoukov.* Bratislava: Slovenské pedagogické nakladateľstvo, 1980.

Krian, George Thomas. *World Education Encyclopedia.* Vol. 1. New York: Facts on File Publications, 1988.

Kucharíková, Anna, Kevin Slavin, and Jozef Galata. *English for Students of Mechanical Engineering.* Bratislava: Slovenská technická univerzita, 2001.

Larson, Jonathan. "Selling Oneself, Selling the Nation: Translating Slovaks for the Eyes of Europe." *Anthropology of East Europe Review* 20, no. 2 (2002). http://condor.depaul.edu/%7Errotenbe/aeer/v20n2/Larson.pdf (accessed June 2, 2006).

Leff, Carol Skalnik. *The Czech and Slovak Republics: Nation versus State.* Boulder: Westview Press, 1997.

Leventis, Stergios, and Pauline Weetman. "Impression Management: Dual Language Reporting and Voluntary Disclosure." *Accounting Forum* 28, no. 3 (2004): 307–28.

Levitt, Stephen, and Steven Dubner. *Freakonomics: A Rogue Economist Explores the Hidden Side of Everything.* New York: HarperCollins, 2005.

Marx, Karl. *Capital.* New York: Penguin, 1976.

Mesežnikov, Grigorij, Miroslav Kollár, and Tom Nicholson, eds. *Slovakia 2002: A Global Report on the State of Society.* Bratislava: Institute for Public Affairs, 2003.

Ministry of Education. "Hodnota maturitnej skúšky dnes a zajtra, alebo 'Nenechajte sa skúšať' dvakrát.'" *Štátny pedagogický ústav,* 2000. http://www .statpedu.sk (accessed January 14, 2006).

"Na bezchybnú angličtinu treba operáciu jazyka." *Sme Online* (message board posting), January 6, 2004. http://www.sme.sk/c/1222207/Na-bezchybnu -anglictinu-treba-operaciu-jazyka.html (accessed April 5, 2007).

Nickerson, Catherine. "English as a *Lingua Franca* in International Business Contexts." *English for Specific Purposes* 24, no. 4 (2005): 367–80.

Pedagogická encyklopédia Slovenska. Volume A–O. Bratislava: Veda, vydavateľstvo slovenskej akadémie vied, 1984.

Pennycook, Alastair. "Beyond Homogeny and Heterogeny: English as a Global and Worldly Language." In *The Cultural Politics of English,* ed. Christopher Mair, 3–18. Amsterdam: Rodopi, 2003.

———. *English and the Discourses of Colonialism.* New York: Routledge, 1998.

Petková, Zuzana. "Vyzradila sa aj maturita angličtiny." *Pravda,* April 5, 2006. http://spravy.pravda.sk (accessed May 30, 2006).

Phillips, Tom. "British Council a reforma maturity na Slovensku." Press release. British Council, April 3, 2000.

Phillipson, Robert. *English-Only Europe? Challenging Language Policy.* London: Routledge, 2003.

———. *Linguistic Imperialism.* Oxford: Oxford University Press, 1992.

———. "Voice in Global English: Unheard Chords in Crystal Loud and Clear." *Applied Linguistics* 20, no. 2 (1999): 265–76.

Popkewitz, Thomas. *Paradigm and Ideology in Educational Research: The Social Function of the Intellectual.* London: Falmer Press, 1984.

Průcha, Jan. "Foreign Language Needs: Theory and Empirical Evidence in Czechoslovakia." Paper presented at the International Testing Symposiums of the Interuniversitare Sprachtestgruppe (IUS), 8th Tampere, Finland, November 17–18, 1984. ERIC Document Reproduction Service No. ED 266 637.

Pytelka, Josef, Anna Janská, and Karel Veselý. *Angličtina pre I. ročník stredných škôl.* Bratislava: Slovenské pedagogické nakladateľstvo, 1969.

———. *Angličtina pre III. ročník stredných škôl.* Bratislava: Slovenské pedagogické nakladateľstvo, 1971.

Radičová, Iveta. "Social Policy." In Mesežnikov, Kollár, and Nicholson, *Slovakia 2002,* 439–58.

Reynolds, Matthew. "Once a Backwater, Slovakia Surges." *New York Times* (business/financial desk late ed.), December 28, 2004.

Rogers, Priscilla S. "International Perspectives on Business Communication Research: National Agendas and the Communication Divide." *Business Communication Quarterly* 61, no. 3 (1998): 79–85.

Roth, Eli, dir. *Hostel.* Lion's Gate, 2006.

Rupert, Mark. *Ideologies of Globalization: Contending Visions of the New World Order.* New York: Routledge, 2000.

Rust, Val. "Educational Responses to Reforms in East Germany, Czechoslovakia, and Poland." *Phi Delta Kappan* 73, no. 1 (1992): 386–89.

Schaffer, Jeff, dir. *Eurotrip.* Dreamworks, 2004.

Schleppengrell, Mary. "Teaching English in Central Europe." Paper presented at the Annual Meeting of the Teachers of English to Speakers of Other Languages, March 1991. ERIC Document Reproduction Service No. ED 333 724.

Simon, Szabolcs, and Miklós Kontra. "Slovak Linguists and Slovak Language Laws." *Multilingua* 19, no. 5 (2000): 73–94.

"Slovak Maturita Seminar on Testing Speaking." Handout. October 27, 2003.

Smith, Adrian. *Reconstructing the Regional Economy: Industrial Transformation and Regional Development in Slovakia.* Cheltenham: Edward Elgar Press, 1998.

Spivak, Gayatri. *A Critique of Postcolonial Reason: Toward a History of the Vanishing Present.* Cambridge: Harvard University Press, 1999.

Stiglitz, Joseph E. *Globalization and Its Discontents.* New York: Norton, 2003.

———. "Information and the Change in the Paradigm in Economics." http://www2.gsb.columbia.edu/faculty/jstiglitz/download/2001_Nobel_Lecture.pdf.

———. "Public Policy for a Knowledge Economy." Remarks at the Department for Trade and Industry and Center for Economic Policy Research, London, January 27, 1999. http://64.233.167.104/search?q=cache:lDKP-35BOdwJ:www.worldbank.org/html/extdr/extme/knowledge-economy.pdf+"public+policy+for+a+knowledge+economy"++Stiglitz&hl=en&ct=clnk&cd=1&gl=us&client=safari.

———. *Whither Socialism?* Boston: Massachusetts Institute of Technology, 1994.

Stiglitz, Joseph E., and Bruce Greenwald. *Towards a New Paradigm in Monetary Economics.* Cambridge: Cambridge University Press, 2003.

Stolarnik, M. Mark. "The Political, Economic, and Cultural Situation in the Slovak Republic (as of May, 1995)." *Slovakia* 37, nos. 68–69 (2003): 172–98.

Švec, Štefan. "Reforming General Education and Teacher Training in Slovakia." *East/West Education* 19, nos. 1–2 (1998–2000): 73–84.

"Those Roamin' Roma." *Economist,* February 7, 2004, 54.

Togneri, Chris. "English—No Longer a Hobby." *Slovak Spectator,* February 8, 1999, 4.

"Transformed." *Economist,* June 25, 2005, 8.

Tridsať rokov socialistického školstva v Československej socialistickej republike, 1945–1975, (II) Stredné školstvo. Praha: Státní pedagogické nakladatelství n. p., 1975.

United Nations Development Programme (UNDP). *Human Development Report 1999.* New York: Oxford University Press, 1999.

Verdery, Katherine. *What Was Socialism, and What Comes Next?* Princeton: Princeton University Press, 1996.

Vodinský, Stanislav. *Schools in Czechoslovakia.* Trans. Till Gottheiner and Joy M. Kohoutová. Prague: State Pedagogical Publishing House, 1965.

Watkins, Evan. *Everyday Exchanges: Marketwork and Capitalist Common Sense.* Stanford: Stanford University Press, 1998.

Wood, Barry D. "Europe's Great Divide." *Barron's,* May 16, 2005, 68.

World Bank. *Doing Business in 2005: Removing Obstacles to Growth.* Washington, D.C.: World Bank, 2005.

———. *The Quest for Equitable Growth in the Slovak Republic: A World Bank Living Standards Assessment.* Report No. 32433-SK. Washington, D.C.: World Bank, 2005.

Zábojová, Eva, Jaroslav Peprník, and Stella Nangonová. *Angličtina I. pre samoukov a kurzy.* Slovak ed. Bratislava: Vydavateľstvo Príroda, s.r.o., 2000.

Index

5506324   h,1/